CHRISTIAN SOCIAL THOUGHT IN GREAT BRITAIN BETWEEN THE WARS

Bruce Wollenberg

University Press of America, Inc.
Lanham • New York • London

BT
738
.W55
1997

Library of Congress Cataloging-in-Publication Data

Wollenberg, Bruce
Christian social thought in Great Britain between the wars / Bruce
Wollenberg.
p.   cm.
Includes bibliographical references.
1. Sociology, Christian--Great Britain--History--20th century. I. Title.
BT738.W55   1996   261.8'0941'09041--dc20   96-34229 CIP

ISBN 0-7618-0495-1 (cloth: alk. ppr.)
ISBN 0-7618-0496-X (pbk: alk. ppr.)

Contents

Chapter 1

Rethinking Church, Rethinking State

Thinkers in interwar Great Britain were engaged in agonized reappraisal of their society. The smooth illusions of prosperity, progress and peace with which they had comforted themselves were shattered by the guns of August, 1914 and they were left, in 1919, with the task of finding a sane way through the despair and confusion remaining in war's wake. What they found eventually was Harold Macmillan's Middle Way, the path to the "responsible," the "compassionate" society, the Welfare State of the 1942 Beveridge Report.

Christian thinkers were part of this quest for a sane way forward. They participated in the formation of, in Auden's phrase, the climate of opinion that made the creation of the Welfare State possible. One emblematic contribution was made by R. H. Tawney. His seminal *Equality* (1931), contends Duncan B. Forrester, "contributed powerfully to the emergence of an egalitarian-welfare consensus in postwar Britain."[1] Tawney based his criticisms and proposals squarely and explicitly on what he considered to be clear Christian, biblical premises, which were shared by his great friend, William Temple. And, like Temple, Tawney had cachet with the public beyond the bounds of the church; although he held belief in God to be a necessary precondition for belief in equality, he was able to frame his arguments in a manner that appealed to many who could not accept their theological underpinnings. In what follows I attempt to show, not that the or a Christian vision triumphed over alternatives, but that Christian thinkers, influencing and influenced by their age, made a contribution to the national dialogue in the course of, concurrently, rethinking the nature of the church and the relationship of what it regarded as its eternal gospel to the social order.

Tawney was deeply indebted to the tradition of English ethical socialism which itself had influenced the public to which he spoke. Thomas More, William Cobbett, L. T. Hobhouse, George Orwell and T. H. Marshall are exemplars of this movement. They had in common a confidence in the fundamental decency of the English people who could be counted on to act morally if they were not brutalized by conditions of poverty and injustice. Orwell compared the nation to a family; Tawney spoke more of fellowship. Both felt that predatory business was being allowed to trample on ideals like the worth of the individual and mutual responsibility.[2] Tawney's ideal for the "free Englishman" (Hobhouse's constant theme) fits well with the tradition of ethical socialism: the fully-developed person in a community which values and sustains cultivated persons.[3]

In their attempt to set forth the elements of what Kant called the ethical commonwealth, Orwell, Tawney and a large number of thinkers in the interwar period were also working in a more specifically Christian tradition of social criticism. A great impetus toward the development of an "ethic of responsibility" in addition to an "ethic of absolute ends" in the church (Weber) had been provided already in the middle years of the nineteenth century by the Christian socialism of Frederick Denison Maurice. Yet the Tractarians before him had also been influential in this regard. Pusey, Newman, *et al.* had invited the English nation to view the English Church as something other than a simple extension of the state. It was to have its own integrity, generated from spiritual sources peculiar to it. Leaven in the social lump, it was to be an agent of God's transforming power. Beholden only to God, the church was to be a school of the soul in which it learned to know and love its Lord. Again, it is my contention that the search for an "ethic of responsibility" should be seen in the context of the Church of England's (and other communions') concern for its identity and integrity in a situation of large-scale flux and upheaval, an ethic that formed the indispensable framework for the Welfare State. True, the Tractarians were far from being social reformers. Yet their concern that the church voice a prophetic, critical and theologically authentic word from God was taken very seriously by many between the wars.

As the nineteenth century wore on, the church found itself, in Bernard M. Reardon's apt phrase, in a "cultural environment no longer disposed to derive its valuations from or pin its hopes to an order of things for which the phenomenal world is but a temporary screen."[4] Industrialization and urbanization had brought in their wake massive social problems which had come increasingly to public attention. Thus the church, many contended, could regard itself as the custodian of an otherworldly, "spiritual" gospel only on peril of becoming terminally marginal. The impetus to recast the church as a prophetic agent of change...or at least to emphasize this role...was strong.

This did not mean, however, that Christian thinkers were forced to adapt wholesale approaches and ideas extant in the secular world. They had at their disposal a rich tradition of social analysis which, in its modern form, derived from Samuel Taylor Coleridge. That tradition can be traced through Maurice, Coleridge's greatest disciple, through J. C. Hare and Thomas Arnold, to T. H. Green and Edward Caird. The latter was hugely influential for several generations of Anglican thinkers, particularly through Charles Gore and his successor in social Christian leadership, William Temple.[5] They imbued their students with a social conscience based on their belief in the Incarnation, the symbol, for them, of God's concern for every aspect of human life.

The Victorian movement toward a more socially aware Christianity was not conducted entirely in the academy. The era saw the appearance of slum priests who had shaped Puseyan and Maurician theological elements into an Anglo-Catholicism that brought ritualistic drama and color to the drabness of places like Portsmouth, Sheffield and Isle of Dogs.[6] Along with the liturgy came a deep commitment to the life of the urban poor in their struggle against poverty, disease and ignorance. The ritualist parsons wrote a heroic chapter in the history of faith-motivated service and in so doing, served notice that at least some elements of the church were unwilling simply to preach paradise to people huddled in pestilential tenements. Although some wrote tracts...H. C. Shuttleworth, for example, and Thomas Hancock...most emphasized action and "social service" rather than engaging in systematic reflection on systemic evils.

Organizations, the "little societies," sprang up to assist the church in revising its understanding of mission in industrialized Great Britain. England's first socialist club, the Guild of St. Matthew, was formed in 1877 by the vicar of Bethnal Green, Stewart Duckworth Headlam. While the Guild many times reflected its flamboyant and eccentric warden, the Christian Social Union, by contrast, tended to be more moderately progressive and inclusive. It supported the emerging Labour Party and numbered Gore, B. F. Westcott and Henry Scott Holland among its membership. Temple met his future spouse while both were officers of the Westminster branch. The CSU's original aim was to formulate a comprehensive Christian political economy, in the sense of a wide-ranging and coherent socio-political theory. This aim was never achieved. The cudgels of comprehensiveness were taken up, however, in the 1930's by the Christendom Group, about which I shall have more to say below. It represents the wildly romantic deviation from the sober middle of church thought that was eventually reflected in post-war legislation.

More like the Guild was the Church Socialist League, strongly identified with the High Church party in the Church of England.[7] It reached its zenith in 1912 and thereafter became fragmented. One of the groups that issued from it was the League of the Kingdom of God, which played an important role in the formation of the Christendom Group.

An analogous Roman Catholic organization was the Catholic Social Guild, begun in 1909 and spearheaded by the well-known Fr. Charles Dominick Plater. He advocated a recovery of the social spirit of the medieval guilds, although, unlike numbers of Anglicans, he did not favor thoroughgoing reinstallation of the guild system. Plater's approach to social problems, typical of the Roman church at the time, was cautious, conservative and non-ideological. His stress was on direct Christian service rather than on drastic change, e. g., along socialist lines.

Anglican societies carried the word socialism in their titles and it was commonly on people's lips in the interwar period. Little consensus about its meaning, however, existed. Angelo Rappoport's 1924 *Dictionary of Socialism* offered thirty-nine definitions[8] and in the years under review in ensuing chapters, Christian thinkers represented several of them. The biblical scholar and famous "Red Dean" of Canterbury, Hewlett Johnson, e.g., remained ever a pilgrim on the uncritical left, an enthusiast for the Bolsheviks and the Soviet government's most tireless Western apologist. For others, like Clive Binyon and Conrad Noel, the leveling, egalitarian impulses of home grown Labour Party socialism were compelling. Temple, on the other hand, while identified with socialist politics all his life, was extremely leery of tethering the reputation of social Christianity to partisan posts. As was the case with Gore, Temple was a socialist of the "soft," ethical type: he liked the notion of public benefit rather than profit as the basic charter for industry; he endorsed socialism's call for fellowship and cooperation rather than capitalist competition to beat at the heart of the economic system. Yet his dialectical cast of mind and his penchant (and gift) for compromise, rendered him indisposed toward any "ism" or ideology.

The word socialism, then, entered the interwar period as it had the Edwardian: a putty-nose word, slippery of definition and owing its ethos more to Cobbett, Robert Owen and William Morris than to Marx and Engels; it remained so through the years between the wars.[9]

Still others, like Maurice Reckitt and Percy Widdrington, while often delivering jeremiads against capitalism and its catastrophes, never embraced a collectivist alternative.[10] Instead, they were long enamored of the politically unrealistic Guild Socialism disdained by Fr. Plater. It seemed to promise all the benefits of interventionist statism with none of its restrictions on individual liberty.[11] Restrictions on individual liberty were very much the concern also of Hilaire Belloc, constantly quoted in the interwar years by religious and secular writers alike. His enormously important book *The Servile State* of 1912 sounded the alarm against abuses of government power and advocated distributism, a decentralized system in which the mass of citizens severally owns the means of production. Belloc's Bruegel-colored glasses were later to be appropriated by the Christendom Group.

Allusion could be made to another universally cited scholar to show that Belloc's romanticism was not universally embraced by those who nevertheless found value in the Middle Ages. J. Neville Figgis, who died in 1919, was an outstanding student of the medieval period, an immensely productive author and a resident of Gore's Mirfield Community, an attempt at injecting the monastic life into the heart of a working class district. His cautiously progressive social criticism was set against a background of meticulous, clear-eyed assessment of medieval achievements and disappointments.

Some thinkers would have nothing to do with any kind of liberal progressivism of whatever historical provenance. A. L. Lilley, close friend of Baron Von Hügel's, was a follower of Tolstoy, with his individualistic anarchism and his notion of the ideal society ruled by love. Like Belloc, he was afraid of overweening state power and was typical of many English Christians who viewed with alarm the infringement of Whitehall into many heretofore private areas of life, a trend that could be seen already at the turn of the century and which accelerated swiftly during World War I. William Cunningham, who died at war's end and was working on a biography of Maurice at the time, argued that the church as such had no business intruding on the affairs of Whitehall. Professor at Cambridge and the founder of economic history as an academic study, he wanted to see material progress "moralized" but not by direct church action: its function should be restricted to the area of moral uplift and does not include dictating "what the Christian millionaire ought to do."[12] He came close to asserting that the "laws" "discovered" by economic science are divine, analogous to the laws of nature. For Cunningham, as for Josiah Stamp in the interwar period, social progress did not follow attempts to contravene these laws with idealistic and, perforce, futile schemes, socialist or otherwise; it occurs spontaneously, osmotically, as increasing numbers of Christians respond to the church's appeal to a higher morality in all of life.[13]

Cunningham's individualistic conservatism put him at odds with one of the most remarkable documents produced by the Church of England in modern times: the so-called Fifth Report. As part of the National Mission of Repentance and Hope,[14] a committee had been formed in 1916 with Dr. Edward Talbot, Bishop of Winchester, as chair and including George Lansbury, Gore and Tawney, who became the Report's chief architect. The committee was charged with outlining the church's best thinking in the areas of worship, evangelism, ecclesiastical government and teaching. Over the ensuing two years reports on these topics were duly issued. Yet it was the fifth in the series, "Christianity and Industrial Problems," that occasioned by far the most heated debate and gained the largest notoriety.

It proposed five principal theses:

- Christian ethics are binding on social relations, not just on individual conduct.
- True wealth lies not in material goods but in the quality of the person.
- Personality is sacred.
- Service is a Christian duty.
- The church should act corporately.

The section of the Report dealing with the historical background of Christian thinking on social issues is a model of balance, lucidity and comprehensiveness. Its evenhanded analysis of the Middle Ages is especially significant in view of the nostalgic and unproductive medievalism to which some were drawn. Its sober realism is reflected in its attempt to chart a course for social theology that avoids the Scylla of enunciating vague moral platitudes, on the one hand and the Charybdis of supporting specific partisan legislation on the other. This search for what came to be called the *media axiomata* position is a key feature of Temple's social thought; it was engaged in extensively by the Life and Work movement and, subsequently, was embraced by the World Council of Churches.[15]

The Fifth Report sounded basic themes...that the economic system should be based on cooperation for public service, not on competition for private gain; that industry should make paying a living wage and providing for adequate leisure its top priorities...that were to echo through the twenties and thirties. It was the charter for the Industrial Christian Fellowship and served as a crucial step in the creation, in 1923, of a permanent Social and Industrial Committee of the Church Assembly. It formed the essential backdrop for the staging of Copec in 1924.[16]

It is difficult to overestimate the importance of the Fifth Report.[17] In issuing it, the English Church set up a milestone on the way to the responsible society and a monument of critical, large-scale thinking prompted by the tenets of religious faith. Not to be superseded in the quality of its writing or in the breadth of its concerns, the Report set the tone and the perimeters of the interwar debate in ecclesiastical circles; and it signaled how difficult would be the task of escaping an enervating theoretical vagueness without identifying the Kingdom's coming with specific laws. If it was flawed, it was because it did not address the tension, lifted up by the Tractarians, between a conception of the church as little more than the nation's conscience and one that viewed it as a divine society whose legitimacy is established theologically, not functionally. Its impact, however, was enormous.

The Fifth Report came out just one month after the Armistice. The Great War, with its devastation and disillusionment had provided a fillip to the quest, already being vigorously pursued, for international and domestic social orders anchored in justice and conducive to peace. Christian participation in this quest naturally reflected the epoch in which it was carried out: it was never "autochthonous."[18] Still, as was the case in the previous century, many interwar people of faith were quite self-consciously attempting, as I have indicated, to construct social theologies resonant with the deepest impulses of the church's theological tradition. And these attempts can be most usefully viewed, in my judgment, as part of a broader, multifaceted process of reform, renewal and rethinking taking place in the church.

We have seen that this process had been going on for some time. It was not without adumbration in the Oxford Movement but its pace quickened in the Victorian era. At that time, evolutionary secularism in general and higher criticism of the Bible in particular were widely regarded by Christians as having taken massive toll on the credibility of the faith. And in stark contrast to medieval times, social and economic development apparently was proceeding along purely secular lines. Thus, twin threats of intellectual indefensibility and cultural irrelevance mobilized Christian minds to reexamine the bases of the faith and the meaning and function of the church.

A notable symbol of that mobilization, one that in its careful examination of many issues of the church's faith and life lies behind the Fifth Report is a volume titled *Lux Mundi*, published in 1889. The book offered essays on a variety of topics by younger churchmen who were convinced that maintaining religion-as-usual would only further erode people's confidence in the church's ability to say anything distinctive or authoritative in the midst of social and intellectual upheaval. The faith once delivered had to be related to the knowledge since discovered. The Light of the world, they believed, had to be refracted through new lenses.

The volume's editor, Charles Gore, felt the challenge keenly and represented in his own career and writings the importance many placed on a *comprehensive* theological reconstruction that did not leave out of account the social, political and economic implications of a thoroughly incarnational understanding of the gospel. *Lux Mundi*'s subtitle was "Essays in the Religion of the Incarnation." For Gore, questions relating to the identity of the church, the articulation and defense of its faith and its role in social criticism and change were bound intimately together. All pointed to a thorough revision of Christianity, felt to be necessary in an age that could no longer accept the scriptures *or* the social order as divinely given in the old straightforward way. Desiring that the church's message be at once authentic and winsome, the editor and his colleagues did their work of drawing out things old and new always with an awareness of the cultured despisers without the church and of souls shaken by modernity within. Yet their appreciation for modern thought, their intellectual integrity and their classically-based humanism did not lead them to ignore the biblical tradition or apostolic proclamation, however historically conditioned they were seen to be. Thus if a Hewlett Johnson or a Kenneth Ingram legitimately could be accused of "playing to the gallery" on occasion, mainstream Christian social thinkers, heavily influenced by Gore, could not. They engaged earnestly, naive and slapdash as their efforts might have been at times, in a search commended to them by Cobbett and Coleridge, by Maurice and Arnold, by Ruskin and Morris: to sketch the outlines of a moral society that provides not only economic rewards and personal freedom but also justice and beauty for all.

The heir to the Fifth Report and *Lux Mundi*, Elisha to Gore's Elijah, was William Temple. With scholarly acumen, ecclesial skill and prophetic zeal, he pressed the case for reform in the church on a number of fronts, including the social. As Gore served as the link between the older "Christian Socialism" and the early part of the twentieth century, so Temple exemplified Christian social thought as it attempted to come to grips with the fear and uncertainty of the twenties and thirties.

A world had died in 1914. What would take its place was anything but clear.

Notes

1. In Geoffrey Wainwright, ed., *Keeping the Faith* (Philadelphia: Fortress Press, 1988), p. 260.

2. Norman Dennis and A. H. Halsey, *English Ethical Socialism* (Oxford: Clarendon Press, 1988), p. 42. Orwell was confirmed by Charles Gore when he was Bishop of Oxford. While Orwell sat lightly on dogma, he could also comment that "one cannot have any worthwhile picture of the future unless one realizes how much we have lost by the decay of Christianity." *Ibid.*, p. 121.

3. *Ibid.*, p. 202.

4. Bernard M. Reardon, *From Coleridge to Gore* (London: Longman, 1971), p. 15.

5. A twentieth century example of this process of Christian return *ad fontes* was Gore's 1913 book *Property*. Its ideas form the basis of Tawney's *The Acquisitive Society* (1921), which reached a wider, "secular" audience.

6. See, e.g., Joseph Clayton, *Father Dolling: A Memoir* (London, 1902). Dolling, an ardent "smells and bells" High Churchman, was a regular speaker at trade unionist meetings and demonstrations and was "full of the spirit of socialism" of an ethical rather than a doctrinaire or ideological type (*ibid.*, p. 65). He spent a year in America, lecturing on social topics and, incidentally, meeting Mary Baker Eddy. He published his own memoir, *Ten Years in a Portsmouth Slum*, in 1896. Dolling died at age 50 in 1901 and quickly became an icon of the Christian socialist movement, the prototype of the dauntless, heroic slum vicar "who worked himself to death for God and his poor." See also Charles E. Osbourne, *The Life of Father Dolling* (London, 1905).

7. Its luminaries included W. E. Moll, Conrad Noel, P. E. T. Widdrington and the famous Leicester slum priest, Lewis Donaldson. The latter is the source of the oft-quoted apothegm "Christianity is the religion of which socialism is the practice."

8. Cited in Ronald H. Preston, *Religion and the Persistence of Capitalism* (London: SCM Press, 1979), p. 4.

9. For a fuller discussion, see Anthony Wright, *British Socialism* (Oxford: Clarendon Press, 1983), pp. 2 ff.

10. In any event, collectivist ideas dominated socialist thought only from the 1880's to about 1912.

11. Striking a balance between individual liberty and collective power was a central concern for Gabriel Gillett, an important Edwardian Christian thinker. His *Politics and Religion* of 1912 was influential and proleptic of much interwar Anglo-Catholic thought.

12. William Cunningham, *Personal Ideals and Social Principles* (London: SPCK, 1919), p. 33.

13. Each in his own way, important men like the Bishop of London throughout the interwar era, Arthur Foley Widdington-Ingram, and Bernard Bosanquet, echoed Cunningham's optimism.

14. This was the Church of England's response to the War and to the drastic decline in influence the church had been experiencing since late Victorian times. Temple was one of its most visible spokesmen. The Mission's spirit of new beginnings could be detected in the Fifth Report; it also lay behind Copec (1924), which placed Temple front and center as a leading interpreter of the church's social thought.

15. This approach has come under attack from the right in recent years. See Ronald H. Preston, *Church and Society in the Late Twentieth Century: The Economic and Political Task* (London: SCM Press, 1983), p. 143. The author offers thoughtful suggestions for the contemporary church's social witness, placing the discussion in historical context, deftly sketched.

16. The Report was reprinted in its entirety in 1927, at which point it had been in continuous circulation, with a distribution of 29,000 copies.

17. Its influence did not wane with the passing years. A major historical review, written by Christendom Group member Philip Mairet in 1956, contains extensive excerpts from the Report, offered as material for contemporary reflection.

18. E. R Norman, in his important *Church and Society in England 1770-1976* (Oxford: Clarendon Press, 1976), displays his palpable disdain for progressive social thinkers...the "socially obsessed" (p. 230)...by locating the source of their ideas in class moralism; they were simply aping the secular intelligentsia. Norman's analog as critic from the right in the interwar period was Herbert Hensley Henson.

Chapter 2

The Twenties

In World War I, says Bentley B. Gilbert, "a world died and a new one was born."[1] This metaphor points more to the prevailing mood than it does to the facts of the case. On Gilbert's own showing, this new world was not a complete *novum* and the continuities between pre-and post-war eras can be readily traced. Yet the international upheaval did create the necessity for change, both in foreign policy and in domestic economic and political arrangements. It also served as the catalyst for nostalgia, thinking about former institutions and ways, a longing for a "return to normalcy" (which was symbolized for many by the serene and decorous George V and politically embodied in Stanley Baldwin).[2] Thus while many felt that *something* must be done to replace or to repair the old order, which had been responsible for the carnage of the Great War, the disruptions and losses of that war rendered them psychologically unprepared to embrace radical, abrupt change. Maurice Reckitt's metaphor for the situation was drawn from American geography: "The War is a sort of Grand Canyon in the history of social and economic theory; and Christians, no less than other social travelers, stood breathless and bewildered upon the edge of that gigantic abyss."[3] For a "breathless and bewildered" nation, then, "the interwar decades were not a period of legislative innovation but a time of adjustment...of legislation worked out in another era from a different set of circumstances."[4]

That indefatigable defender of liberalism, C. F. G. Masterman, considered the condition of his country in *England After War* and painted a pessimistic picture, comparing his analysis to the one he had published fourteen years previous. "The world of which I then wrote," wrote Masterman, "has vanished."[5] He could see no good having come from the war. Economic stability was gone, the Versailles treaty had no friends and the dominant mood was one of fear. He predicted, accurately, a continuation of the wartime strife between capital and labor, the palliative efforts of the churches being "futile and dim"

The masses were staggering, numb. "Men and women," he reported, "move like phantoms in a dying world," uninterested in anything.[6] And the poets? They were all bitter.[7]

A new class was emerging: the "new poor." Its members were drawn from the ranks of the middle class which Masterman saw as under economic attack. A sure sign was the letting go of domestic help, a trend which would accelerate greatly after 1929. Immediately after the war, however, the almost universal mark of the middle class was the employment of live-in servants.[8] Britain had entered the war a creditor nation and emerged from it a debtor, forced off the gold standard in order to attempt to meet its obligations. The most serious problem was the disruption of the country's export trade, caused by its overinvestment in the heavier, "staple" industries and by stiffened competition from abroad.[9] This situation placed great strains on a heretofore fairly secure middle class, which now found itself crouching between the demands of profiteer and proletariat. Masterman was especially angered by the former, who had taken unfair advantage of the nation during the war; he devoted an entire chapter to the subject. Goldsmith, in another generation, warned of the nation's need to strengthen its "bold peasantry;" in 1922, Masterman found himself penning an extended lament for the middle class, workers of "pen and brain."[10]

The urbanized successors to Pope's peasantry had benefitted from the boomlet of 1920-21 but the seeds of its destruction were already sown in rising government borrowing rates, advancing unemployment and plummeting prices.[11] Already the debilitating effects of the dole could be observed. Working class people, particularly the returning soldiers, were disillusioned, yet they were not inclined to turn to radical ideologies; their attraction to the new Labour Party was not based on philosophy but on their desire to have what the rich had. Only the intelligentsia moved left while the upper classes occupiedd themselves with "frivolous pursuits."[12]

Masterman saw the churches in the doldrums, despite the recently concluded Life and Liberty movement and the Fifth Report in the Church of England, with the masses indifferent (the only "preacher" who got through to people was H. G. Wells, whom Masterman, not surprisingly, regarded as perhaps the most influential man alive). Most ecclesiastical leaders were old, he noted and no new leaders had emerged to galvanize new crusades. His overly-harsh judgment on the bishops: mediocre.[13] This assessment might have been colored by the prelates' perceived disinclination wholly to support Masterman's enthusiasm and apologetic for the centrist Liberal Party.

His enthusiasm also embraced the old Westcott-Scott Holland, Christian Social Union tradition, which he saw persisting in the work of ecclesiastical art historian and liturgiologist Percy Dearmer. Masterman was impressed with the well-attended Sunday evening Guildhall services Dearmer was conducting with A. Maude Royden, at which the concerns of the poor were consistently lifted up. He had little use for the Anglo-Catholic left, dismissing Conrad Noel as the proprietor of his "Cathedral Church at Thaxted." The focus of attention, Masterman reported, was on the modernists and their controversial critical theology. This contentious orientation of the Church was unfortunate, he felt, because it deflected attention away from the concern's of society's needy. Reflecting the interest in ecclesiology which I find a *leitmotiv* in Christian social thinking between the wars, Masterman rued that that Church as a corporate entity had been negligent in "setting up the banner of Social Righteousness." In its search for a return to the supposed calm of the *status quo ante bellum*, the State was inclined to try to ignore the problems created by social and economic inequity. The Church had a duty to compel the State to "face realities" but had not, e.g., spoken out on the rash of post-war strikes that "have left a legacy of bitterness which will last long."[14]

In sum, where some had anticipated a revival of faith, Masterman observed only cessation of belief along with a residual and "desperate desire for communication with the dead." "The tide of the spirit runs low" is his concluding comment in his stylishly written, melancholy survey of the immediate post-war period.[15]

A prominent leader in social Christian circles at this time was a layman, Will Reason. His book of 1919, *Christianity and Social Renewal*, contained a forward by Charles Gore and foreshadowed Copec in its list of interests. For Reason, the post-war watchword was Reconstruction along the lines that were discernible before 1914. The poor for some time had been advancing educationally and this fact, coupled with the wider diffusion of information, allowed many of the working class clearly to recognize the disparity between their style of life and that of the more well-off. In addition, they were more capable of organizing themselves to achieve political goals than had previously been the case. As it plays its role in the great drama of Reconstruction, said Reason, the church's function will be to provide "guiding principles and compelling motives."[16] The principles would be Truth, Righteousness, and Goodwill, i.e., those of the Kingdom of God; the motives would be grounded in the Gospel and include loyalty to the King and a disposition to regard all people as brothers for whom Christ died.

Reason, noting the expansion of the sphere of government influence in peoples' lives during the war, voiced again Belloc's fear of the coming of the "servile state" and seemed to identify socialism with the advance of this supervening power of the collectivity. This kind of power is held illegitimately because its liberty-curtailing effect contravenes the true nature of the state, which is to serve as an "organ of ministry to the common life," Reason contended.[17]

The quality of that common life, he suggested, anticipating the Lambeth Report of the following year, was severely compromised by the lack of provision for a living wage and he quoted the ever-quoted Seebohm Rowntree (as did the Report) on the shocking number of people living below even a conservatively drawn poverty line. Reason's concerns in response to this intolerable situation were those of many Christians in the interwar years: machines are idle because their products can't be disposed of; humans are treated as "hands"; workers are inadequately housed and leisure opportunities are few, with the exception of the public house (a favorite theme of conservative Christian commentator A. C. Headlam); unemployment is not a simple phenomenon but brings a host of related problems in its wake, such as strife in the family, alcohol abuse and gambling.

Reason's book was not without its quirks: he suggested, e.g., that if workers were provided with recreational facilities near their homes, their interest in excursions would decrease and, hence, some "necessary" Sunday labor (work on excursion trains, e.g.) would disappear.[18] On the whole, however, it was a rather pedestrian commentary on social problems, weak both in theology and in offering practical proposals for "Christian Social Reconstruction," although it did contain a listing of the principles and proposals agreed upon by the Interdenominational Conference of Social Service Unions. Its secretary was Lucy Gardner, who was to play a prominent role in Copec and included in its membership Baptist, Anglican, Congregational, Friends, Methodist, Presbyterian, Roman Catholic and Unitarian churches (and the Student Christian Movement).

Generally "progressive" in tone, *Christianity and Social Renewal* advanced notions which could have offended few and which had to wait until Copec to be deepened and fleshed out.

Robert Graves and Alan Hodge characterized the decade as the "careless twenties" and it did seem that most people couldn't have cared less about anything beyond restoring normalcy to their private lives.[19] Certainly a return to the profounder things of the spirit, much hoped-for by the chaplains who, presumable, had failed to find any atheists in the foxholes or trenches, failed to materialize. Demobilized soldiers laid aside their combat Christianity along with their uniforms; for them, "God as an all-wise Providence was dead; blind Chance succeeded to the Throne."[20] One of the few of those returning chaplains able to arouse any pious passion post-war was the famous Woodbine Willie, Geoffrey Studdert Kennedy. He had gained popularity with the troops through his comradely, down-to-earth style: he earned his sobriquet by offering a "Woodbine" cigarette along with encouraging pastoral words.

Upon his return to England after the war, he began to criss-cross the country, preaching to large and enthusiastic crowds in a dynamic, forceful style. As a traveling secretary for the newly-formed Industrial Christian Fellowship, Studdert Kennedy brought a message that was never narrowly "evangelistic," but aimed at social as well as personal renovation. He supported the labor movement, although he refrained from joining the nascent Part, regarding the cause of the working class as transcending partisan interests. "God is the great politician," he declared, and the church ought to recognize that it and the labor movement have aims and ideals in common.[21] Both are concerned with winning freedom for the oppressed and with affirming the dignity and infinite value of each individual. Employing racy language ("bamboozled"), Studdert Kennedy argued against the rhetoric of class war and, during the "Red Years" 1919-21, urged the burial of Marx: he was "not really a prophet."[22] Possessed of a lively, well-trained intellect, he was more the moralist than the social philosopher, sounding at times like William Morris in his denunciation of the cheap, vulgar products and forms of entertainment of which the masses were enamored. A prominent feature of Studdert Kennedy's stump theology was its thoroughgoing sacramentalism. His appeals for social justice were laced with references to the Eucharist, in which Christ gives life freely to all and which establishes a fellowship of love and mutual support, the antithesis of self-interest. "Sweat," he said, "is sacramental wine poured in service of God's world."[23] Studdert Kennedy, as was claimed about a number of other preachers of social righteousness in previous generations, wore himself out with work and went to an early grave.[24]

Studdert Kennedy began no movement of his own. He served, rather, the ICF, which was promoting the principles laid down in the Fifth Report; he had also served part-time with Life and Liberty with his fellow-chaplain Dick Sheppard. Chaplains Neville Talbot and Philip "Tubby" Clayton, however, founded an institution that endured after the war. Talbot House (known by its signaler's shorthand name, Toc H) had been established in a rented house near Ypres in 1915 as a club for soldiers and functioned as a "home away from home" within a religious framework. Back home, Toc H was sponsored by the Prince of Wales and received a Royal Charter in 1922.[25] Branches were established throughout the country in the interwar years and, while it attempted to foster fellowship across class lines and upheld the ideal of community service, the Toc H movement did not develop a systematic Christian critique of society.

The class barrier had long been a concern of social progressives. The gender barrier, attacked with passion and even violence in the pre-war years, remained as an object of Christian scrutiny after the war. The leading feminist in the Anglican Church throughout the period was A. Maude Royden, who had been at the forefront of Life and Liberty. She was a leader not only because of her prominence and her unflagging zeal in support of progressive causes but also because she had a mind easily the equal of the finest of her male counterparts. In 1920, the League of the Church Militant brought out a pamphlet titled *History or Antiquarianism?* which was Royden's incisive analysis of a recent debate on the subject of women in the Lower House of Convocation and the subsequent Report of the Archbishop. The worthies, she wrote, cite tradition as the basis for excluding females from expanded roles in church and society. Yet their citations are extremely selective; why aren't they consistent, she asked, and urge believers to follow the apostolic injunctions about kosher food in Acts 15:19? Her argument is that the authentic tradition of the church conduces to the breaking down of barriers between people; its *Tendenz* is toward equality. Christ himself points the way from revenge through justice to mercy. To assert male dominance on traditional bases, therefore, is not traditionalism at all, but obfuscating antiquarianism!

A similarly astute pamphlet, *Women and Theology*, also published by the League, came from Royden's pen in the same year. This tract demonstrates that there was some first-rate thinking being done in a time of rife intellectual confusion. It also shows that its author was in advance both of her times and of the church of the times. In language not unlike that of contemporary feminist writers, Royden underscored the point that women's experience is different from men's. To deprive society of the benefits of the insights women can bring to the business of living is unfairly and stupidly to deprive everyone. In theology, e.g., where men see God as a king, with people as subjects, women will tend to envision a father, whose "kingdom" is his children's home. Many think, she reported, that the section of Luke's Gospel containing the Prodigal Son pericope was supplied by a woman.

The Rev. F. M. Green contributed a 1920 League of the Church Militant tract titled *The Case Re-Stated* and it, too, contained clear, cogent argumentation. Like Royden, Green looked to authentic tradition as a weapon for equality: the modern trend of women's advance is "a corollary of the truth which the Church has proclaimed for centuries." In his earthly ministry the Lord bestowed on women a status and dignity that was nothing short of revolutionary. The fact that he appointed no female apostles was culturally conditioned and not a sufficient reason for barring them from the priesthood. Paul was likewise limited by his epoch from applying his own principles of equality. Therefore it is important for the church to distinguish between unconditional catholic principle and temporally conditioned custom. Although Green could discern the Spirit of God in what even at that pre-Friedan time he could call the "women's movement," procedural caution was advisable. The church was not, in his judgment, ready to consider opening Orders to women. But an important first step would be the opening of all lay ministries to them.

The 1920 Lambeth Conference, moving in the direction charted by Green, had canonically restored the office of Deaconess and this was celebrated in still another tract, *The Coming Clergy-Woman* by Edith Picton-Turbervill, OBE. The pamphlet was somewhat mistitled: it was not a defense of women's ordination but merely an endorsement of the bishops' move to bring women into more prominent leadership positions in the church.[26] The Lambeth Conference was notable for taking social and ethical questions more seriously than its predecessors.[27] It took up the issue of contraceptives, e.g., declaring that their use was justified only under "abnormal circumstances." This view would come to be modified considerably in the years following.[28]

Lambeth 1920 expressed strong support for the League of Nations, a position that was highly popular in Great Britain at the time. A. C. Headlam was disturbed, however, by what he regarded as the bishops' intellectual fuzziness at the Conference and by their tendency to fall back into pacifism. He was also dismayed that the League charter did not provide for strong sanctions, including military measures, to be applied to offending states.[29]

The year 1920 marked the formation of the Communist Party of Great Britain, which was to attract no Christian and, indeed, little support of any kind in the years that followed. There was also a tiny Socialist Party of Great Britain which had broken with the Social Democratic Federation in 1904. The colorful men who ran the party were zealously occupied with doctrinal purity and theoretical clarity; they wrangled ceaselessly among themselves and distanced their party from all others. Rigidly dogmatic, they regarded religion as the antithesis of socialism. Their story is engagingly told by Robert Barltrop in *The Monument* (London: Pluto Press, 1975). There was much labor unrest at this time, mostly in the transportation industry. Ernest Bevin earned the title "the dockers' KC) and, riding a wave of popular working class support for the Russian Revolution, blocked the loading of the "Jolly George." It was to have carried munitions to forces hostile to the Bolsheviks. Impending violence closer to home was signaled by passage of the Government of Ireland Act and by the recruitment of the notorious 'Blacks and Tans" contingent of ruffians, many of them ex-soldiers.

A book of major importance for the social Christian movement was published at this time. Bearing an introduction by R. H. Tawney, who was to publish his own classic the following year, it was written by Charles Gore and titled *Christianity Applied to the Life of Men and of Nations*. The author based his argument on a conception of the church which does away with the dualism he felt permeated ecclesiastical thinking. Religion has a message for society as well as for the individual, Gore declared. By thus asserting the right of the church to raise its voice in the councils of the powerful, he at once earned the scorn of those inside and outside the church who thought it should not speak corporately on matters material.

In the first instance, Gore claimed, Christianity is a life: practical, moral and unspeculative. This life ought to be reflected by the institutions and customs of society. When it isn't...when, e.g., a morally flaccid cultus draws attention away from the necessity for ethical renewal and transformation...then God sends prophets who, like Jesus, denounce injustice and economic oppression.[30] And, he observed, the primitive Christian community strove for economic justice within its ranks: it could be viewed as "frankly socialist in spirit," even when allowance is made for the tendency in church history to idealize the communal life of the early church.[31] His socialistic attitude may have colored his own view of the first century, however, and under the influence of pre-war Continental liberal scholarship, he was able to assure his readers that "It is a beautiful and reassuring picture which history presents to us;" the life of the early Christians "really represents the ideal of Christ practically realized."[32]

If Gore was slightly soft on the believers of old, his analysis of the latter day saints was not. The church, he said, "has sacrificed reality to numbers" and, under the influence of a Hellenized intellectualism, nationalization of Christianity and the "Romanizing" notions of easy salvation and inquiry-free acceptance of dogma, has allowed people to regard themselves as Christians without serious moral effort. Thus the important analytical and prescriptive work being done by J. L. and Barbara Hammond, e.g., could not be seconded and extended by the English Church.

The apologetical theme, prominent in *Lux Mundi*, emerged again. Gore noted the almost universal revolt against Christianity, fomented by intellectual difficulties and by post-war sexual laxity but also exacerbated by the church's perceived preference for the rich and powerful.[33] Gore in his long ministry participated intensively in the attempt to present to the inquiring mind an intellectually respectable Christianity and, while he was loath to lower the church's sexual standards to attract more moderns, he did grant critics the point that the church displayed more concern for itself than for the poor and the powerless. He did not, however, espouse the old "justify God to the people" theodicy line, with its implication that the long-alienated working class would move closer to the national church if it could be seen to be supporting causes other than those favored by the rulers. For Gore, faithfulness to the tradition took precedence over its attractive presentation to the skeptical and the disaffected. If real Christianity would be preached, a Christianity that engaged in a critique of all temporal schemes and institutions from a timeless perspective, it would be no more popular among the laboring folk than it would be among capitalists, he argued. Inge had warned of the dangers of "playing court chaplain to King Demos," currying favor by means of a divisive and ill-considered apologetic; Gore, for his part, warned of the danger of the church losing its soul by courting any class. Still, he was unable to remain entirely neutral: true preaching, he suggested, will identify us with the principles of the Labour Movement at its best."[34]

Gore's comments on the international scene included a fairly optimistic assessment of the armistice and of the League, the latter reflecting the "supranational spirit" of Christianity. Yet he joined the growing number of people who had abandoned naive hopes for the League, wondering how it could keep the peace without a genuine repudiation of the nationalism evident among its members. Gore also supported the ecumenical movement gaining force at the time. There ought to be constructed, he wrote, an alliance of the churches parallel to the League which would stand for social justice (he mentioned specifically the emancipation of women). The Life and Work idea "Doctrine Divides, Service Unites" appeared here but without the slogan.

Thus in 1920 Gore was continuing to press for a comprehensive, apologetically aware theology that would take seriously both the claims of the best scholarship on the mind and the claims of the poor on the heart.

That year also saw the birth of *The Pilgrim*, "A Review of Christian Politics and Religion," with William Temple as editor. Its purpose, similar to that of another journal of the time, *The Challenge*, was stated in its inaugural issue: "A religion which offers no solution to world-problems fails to satisfy; a scheme of reconstruction, apart from religion, strikes cold and academic. Our effort is to bring home to men the claim of Christ that He is the Way, the Truth and the Life."[35] Temple had been approached by the publisher R. G. Longman to undertake the editorship, which he accepted while Canon of Westminster and in which he continued, as Bishop of Manchester, until the quarterly's demise in 1927.

In its initial number Temple joined many others in applauding the leadership of the bishops at the Lambeth Conference, with special reference to their work on international and industrial matters. They had given impetus, he wrote, to the process of finding ways to "evangelize international politics and christen the industrial system." More specific suggestions as to how these goals might be reached were promised for later issues. This first issue carried an article on "Mysticism, Philosophy and Religion" by Temple's constant critic, Dean Inge, as well as one by his good friend and supporter, the brilliant O. C. Quick, who served as book review editor.[36] There were reviews of books by Laski, Tawney and C. D. H. Cole and a short essay on Christian unity by the editor.

Christian unity was also on the mind of E. G. Selwyn, who commented on its "ever-growing" importance in the premier issue of *Theology* (July, 1920). This journal did not have *The Pilgrim*'s twin foci of religion and politics but it did comment, on occasion, on affairs of the day. It, too, lauded Lambeth 1920, singling out for special praise its thinking on marriage, contraception and divorce, which Selwyn and author Mary Scharlieb judged more positive and clear than that of the 1908 conference. The journal carried a warm but noncommittal appreciation of C. E. Raven's *Christian Socialism* and, noting its need for the "Christian spirit," welcomed the League of Nations. In the July-December, 1920 number, T. W. Pym favorable reviewed "The Church and Social Service," the report issued by a committee appointed by the Archbishop of Canterbury to suggest ways for the church to respond to the Fifth Report. Thus even a journal not primarily concerned with "social Christianity" welcomed it, suggesting that it was quite proper for the church to cooperate with the state in eliminating social evils. Pym went so far as to advocate using tax money to pay for child care in support of working mothers, an idea clearly in advance of its time. It should be noted that an article like Pym's should not be seen as an indicator that a socially passionate and politically sophisticated outlook had suddenly replaced the old "spiritualized" individualism and moralism. That was not the case. The Guild of St. Matthew had not finally triumphed on the pages of *Theology*. What it and *The Pilgrim* show, rather, is that the idea of the "responsible society"[37] was growing slowly, like a sprouting seed, in the soil of church and nation. But before that sprout could come to full flower, the British people were to go through a period in which the maturing pains would be acutely felt.

As William Temple rightly observed, "in 1920 the great disillusionment was just beginning.[38]

By 1921, the post-war economic upswing was beginning a downturn, accompanied by bitter labor disputes. The early spring saw a revived Triple Alliance (miners, railway and transport workers) attempting concerted action, culminating in "Black Friday," April 15, when only the miners, however, went out. This initiated a period of union amalgamations which, in the event, were not able to stave off a crushing labor defeat in the General Strike of 1926. Unemployment, at the forefront of the nation's concern in the thirties, was already emerging as a major source of social unrest. Raids on factories were held, with the raiders demanding a stoppage of work until the management guaranteed higher wage rates. There were mass demonstrations in northern England, in Scotland and in Wales and the grievances of the unemployed were made known in the capital, in October, when 40,000 of the laid-off marched on Trafalgar Square. The protest was organized by Wal Hannington, a well-known unionist and communist agitator throughout the period. It was marked by brutal beatings visited on the workers by the police.[39]

The response of the Upper House of Canterbury Convocation to industrial unrest was to stage a full-dress debate on the subject, with primary attention given to the coal industry. A resolution calling on industry to recognize payment of a living wage as its most fundamental obligation was put forward but not voted on; the bishops contented themselves with Fifth Reportish generalities about the Christian spirit of commerce. The League of Nations received solid support.[40] And substantial time was spent in discussing the role of women in the church. This was also the year in which the Archbishops appointed a Commission on Christian Doctrine, of which William Temple became a member in 1923 and chair in 1925. Its report was finally published in 1938.

Temple was consecrated Bishop of Manchester in 1921 and in that year a young Anglo-Catholic priest, Basil Jellicoe, came to the fetid London slum known as Somers Town. He became for the twenties and thirties what Fr. Robert Dolling had been for an earlier period: the prototypical High Church parson who worked himself into nervous exhaustion and premature death in ministry to the poor. Many people who were not otherwise sympathetic to social Christianity cheerfully supported Jellicoe and made his "non-partisan" movement for decent housing one of the most popular and effective in the interwar years. Temple called him a saint.[41]

Jellicoe had studied at Magdalen College, then served in the Royal Navy during the War, at which time he came under the influence of Studdert Kennedy, although they never met. When he had completed his theological studies he was sent to Somers Town and the mission his *alma mater* had established there. As a priest attached to St. Mary's Church, he ingratiated himself with the neighborhood youth, winning them with smiles and songs, accompanying himself on the accordion. The further he became involved in the life of the parish, the more appalled he became at the wretched conditions in which the people lived. Flat after flat he found to be too small for the number of people who were living in them; the walls were perpetually damp and vermin-infested, the plumbing inadequate, heat and light scarce.

Jellicoe founded the St. Pancras House Improvement Society in 1924 with £250. The Archbishop of Canterbury became its patron and its advisory council boasted such well-known names as Henry Slesser (who later became a Roman Catholic) and Sidney Dark. The Society promoted its work of urban renewal by placing ads in church publications, by publishing *Housing Happenings* and *The War Whoop* and by sending out the tireless Jellicoe himself to plump for the cause. His message was very much colored by Anglo-Catholic sacramental theology, with its Maurician stress on the Incarnation. The church, he said, must work to make the love of God take material shape in the lives of the poor, rather than limiting itself to a spiritualized, otherworldly appeal. We are all, he declared, "blood relations of the King of Kings," who was born in a rude manger and who had a special concern for those caught in analogous situations.[42]

In addition to his serious and successful housing work, Jellicoe engaged in more flamboyant gestures, such as opening a pub, The Anchor, in 1929. Its purpose was to offer social services and religious counseling along with the food and drink. It did not achieve notable success and, in 1933, the Society asked Jellicoe, who demonstrated clear signs of being a manic-depressive, to step aside. In that same year he became involved with the League of the Kingdom of God and went to work for the Isle of Dogs Society, similar in purpose to the St. Pancras organization. His League involvement represented a departure from his usual pattern, which was to ignore theory in favor of addressing the pressing social problems at hand. But his contacts with Anglo-Catholic thinker P. E. T. Widdrington and others brought him more and more into the orbit of those whose theological analyses of society were broadly conceived and productive of comprehensive visions.

One of the most influential thinkers of this type was R. H. Tawney. In 1921 he published one of his most important books, *The Acquisitive Society*, parts of which had been brought out previously by the Fabian Society. It has the flavor of a tract or sermon and argues that the nation "has stumbled upon one of the turning points in history."[43] Too much emphasis is placed on productivity, while "moral principles are what the prophets of this dispensation despise." This present state of affairs is contrasted by Tawney with the "sublime, if too much elaborated, synthesis" that shaped the Middle Ages. Tawney, however, was no medieval escapist; his references to the "catholic wholeness" of the period were always made in the service of an energetic optimism, rather than of a deadening historicism, which sought practical social gains based on enduring principles.

In Tawney's mind, these principles, conducive to social cohesion, had been largely lost sight of by 1700, when private rights, rather than the common welfare, came to occupy center stage. Liberalism, that "fighting creed" of Laski's[44] had been, in the hands of those who had imbibed the reforming spirit of Bentham and the radicals, an instrument of positive economic and political change. Now, however, wrote Tawney, it is being used by the "business aristocracy to bind insurgent movements on the part of an immigrant and semi-servile proletariat."[45] During the war, e.g., the coal owners denounced any restrictions on profits as robbery. This attitude presumes the belief that economic rights are anterior to and independent of economic function. This is wrong. In place of the Acquisitive Society, in which expediency rules, Tawney proposed to erect the Functional Society, in which human values would reign. On the way to such a society, Tawney suggested abolishing "those types of private property in return for which no function is performed," like urban ground-rents and royalties.[46] Industrial producers would be directly responsible to the community through their immediate subordination to shareholders, whose goal is service. Tawney felt that when economic activity was organized around the principle of service, society would disincline toward war and he was highly critical of those "ruining the vanquished" with a harsh peace treaty. Over Versailles he saw written "the Macht-Politik of the Acquisitive Society, the natural, if undesired, consequence of which is war."[47]

Tawney was also highly critical of a Christianity cut off from social responsibility. If society is a "community of wills" which can be inspired to common ends, then the function of the churches is to propagate, he wrote, "the social ethics of the New Testament" (he seemed to assume that the New Testament in this regard is univocal and readily grasped). The Church of England, he complained, has become the "servile client of a half-pagan aristocracy" and thus neutralized as the nation's conscience.[48] The Nonconformists were no better: they were individualistic both in piety and in social morality. Tawney did not get much farther than this in shaping a social theology. He did advert to the church's teaching that all people are equal under a single Creator, a stock social gospel premise. They are to be viewed as derivative being and therefore their rights are conditional, not absolute. Serving the common weal, not stacking up possessions, should be their major mode. Economic and political activity were regarded by Tawney as somehow sacramental, to be judged by the highest standards. What is needed in the church is a recovery of authority, although he did not say how this is to be accomplished, other than urging its members to adopt a "rule of life." He did imply that the word "Christendom" lacked meaning to his contemporaries, a factor that was sometimes overlooked by his contemporaries later in the decade, who coupled the recovery of authority with a return to something approximating the medieval synthesis. In the search for a straight path through the tortuous years ahead, the issue of authority would continue to be important, if not always acknowledged.

Tawney was not dispassionate; he could harumph and fulminate and in an important sense, *The Acquisitive Society* is a tract. It reveals its author's genuine passion, informed by his Christian faith, for a revolution in attitude or, as we might say, in "consciousness" based on the soundest social analysis and on humane assumptions. With this "paradigm shift" (again, as we might call it), a new kind of Christian civilization could be formed to replace the old, wrecked one, a social order in which industry would treat people as people, not as "hands" and which, itself moral, would serve as an ethical pedagogue to its citizens. Tawney in 1921 affirmed the classical vision: not only a reformed society but a society that reforms.[49]

Stanley Pierson suggests that by the early twenties, socialism was no longer a cause, a revolutionary movement for a new order, but a program of social reform.[50] Yet some nostalgia for an earlier, more urgent socialism is evident in G. Clive Binyon's *The Christian Faith and the Social Revolution*, published in 1921. For the author, there was indeed such a thing as the International Socialist Movement based on moral principles and with a social realism practically identical to that to which the church was committed. Unfortunately, polarization existed: socialists equate religion with reaction while believers identify socialism with secularism.[51] This, of course, was true and demonstrated how little substantial impact the Christian socialists from the days of Maurice had had on the British people. For these practical-minded, non-ideological folk, socialism could be sold only in its "soft," ethical form and not as a comprehensive revolutionary package, especially if it were of foreign provenance. If Sir William Harcourt could say, at the onset of the decade, "we are all socialists now,"[52] he could not have meant that the Bolshevik Revolution was imminently to become the model for England's post-war reconstruction. He could only have been alluding to the building consensus that the solution to massive social and economic problems could no longer be left to chance or to charity but would have to be found collectively. The result of this consensus was not institutional transformation but the installation of social security in the Welfare State.

The building of that consensus was being abetted in 1921 by Christians such as Binyon. He offered, out of the socialist kit-bag, the notion of economic life marked by cooperation, not competition, as an important nexus of agreement for progressive people, socialist or not. And, indeed, the phrase did seem to have charm, vague and alliterative as it was, to woo many to its circle, even the distinguished and hardly socialist Josiah Stamp. Binyon was capable of sounding militant: what is required is Revolutionary, not Evolutionary Socialism; the socialist spirit is "a continuous approximation towards communistic anarchism,"[53] but the substance of his recommendations differed little from the Fifth Report and, as I have pointed out in reference to the Report, that substance became standard fare in interwar social Christian preaching. He invoked the Holland-Gore argument about private property (right to it is secondary, contingent); he praised St. Thomas for his insistence on a just price; and he plumped for a national minimum in wages, housing and leisure.[54] As for the class war urged on the proletariat by certain sections of the "International Socialist Movement," its real import becomes, for Binyon, nothing more than socialist carrying on the fight for social justice.[55]

A socialist in only the loosest sense of the word, the Bishop of Manchester

kept social justice issues clearly in view in the pages of *The Pilgrim*. He did
not find the national government assiduously pursuing equality of economic
opportunity in 1921; rather, he saw opportunism on the wartime model
rampant and political life at its lowest moral level ever.[56] He did praise,
however, the terms of the coal settlement, which had been hammered out
in response to a serious miners' strike and the subsequent declaring of a
state of emergency. What was required by way of prevention, Temple
asserted, was the promotion of fellowship in industry, a theme that recurs
frequently in his *Pilgrim* writing and elsewhere. And this promotion is one
of the main tasks of Christianity, he said, without going into practical detail.

The Irish problem continued to trouble the nation[57] and Temple, not an
uncritical Sinn Fein supporter, nevertheless criticized British reprisals in
Ulster as excessive and nominated as unchristian the idea that Ireland ought
to be retained in the Empire at all costs. "Ireland," he wrote in April, 1921,
"still challenges us with the question whether, when we conquered the
bodies of the Prussians, Prussianism conquered our souls." Temple joined
many in decrying the vindictiveness of the Paris Peace Conference. It was
a mistake to make Germany a tributary for more than a generation, with no
attempt at reconciliation; besides, he noted, "there is no prospect that the
terms settled at Paris will be enforced through all the weary years that they
contemplate."[58]

Again on the domestic front, Temple took notice of the unemployment
problem and looked toward a time when each industry would take
responsibility for its workers, thereby eliminating the dole. Industrial
fellowship of this sort seemed to be emerging in Italy and Temple thought
it could be a model for Great Britain and historically more important than
the Russian Revolution. In this connection he could speak of a
"Christianized industrial order" and point toward some form of Guild
Socialism, an idea soon to suffer a large decline in popularity, as necessary
for its realization.

Reflecting its editor's catholic sympathies, *The Pilgrim* opened its pages
to writers of various theological stripes. The distinguished Nonconformist
social thinker and ecumenist A. E. Garvie wrote on "Common Christian
Conscience," with W. L. Knox representing Anglo-Catholicism and
Anthony C. Deane arguing the case for the Broad Church, objecting to the
fact that in recent times "Broad Church" had been narrowed in connotation
to "Modernist."[59] This was written in the year in which the critical
Modernist Conference was held at Girton College, Cambridge, and which
C. L. Mowat cites as the high point of the persuasion's influence.[60] It
produced little social thought and was shortly to be overtaken by a healthy,

no-longer-defensive Anglo-Catholicism that provided a congenial theological home for many social thinkers between the wars.[61]

Enthusiasm for social issues was not limited to Anglicanism and the March, 1921 number of *Theology* took note of that summer's ecumenical Student Christian Movement conference at Glasgow. It attracted 2,400 students who considered such topics as racism in India and heard J. H. Oldham and William Temple, as well as R. H. Tawney on industrial problems and Viscount Grey on the already hoary topos, cooperation versus competition in economic life. The journal was primarily concerned with theology along narrow, academic lines. Yet it is a measure of the importance many attached to social thought at the time that it gave over space to an A. W. Kirkaldy, who wrote an article, inoffensive and inconclusive, on "Industrial Ideals" or to a Bishop of Winchester, writing on Henry Scott Holland. *Theology* was essentially cautious in this area, however, and its articles tended toward the vague, the general and the bland.

Perhaps a book representative of the year 1921 is Maurice L. Rountree's *Social Freedom*, published by the Society of Friends. Like many, he was enthusiastic about Guild Socialist ideas, quoting G. D. H. Cole extensively and citing what came to be the signal and almost only success the Guildsmen could point to: the cooperative experiment at Walthamstow. Stating that he held no brief for Major Douglas' Social Credit scheme, Rountree nevertheless quoted several articles in the journal *New Age* and his own interviews with Douglas and with editor A. R.. Orage. This scheme, which was to be seconded by no mainstream thinkers, was to wield an uncanny power over the minds of a number of interwar Christian writers, about which I will have more to say below. By the thirties, the Social Credit proposal was being touted shrilly as the savior of civilization. In 1921, however, in a time of cautious optimism reflected in Rowntree's book, it was put forward as but one idea useful to a society going about the business of careful reconstruction. Rountree's earnest essay contained examples of solid biblical exegesis and large blocks of material from Walter Rauschenbusch's *Christianizing the Social Order.* Yet overall it was eclectic, ragged and random, presaging the confusion that would be a feature of some Christian social thought as tension increased and optimism faded.

In this discussion I am focussing chiefly on the Anglican Church. It was the ecclesiastical home for the Westcotts and Scott Hollands, the Gores and Temples, the Oldhams and Demants, the influential, high-profile performers on the national stage. Thorough attention to it is necessary for an understanding of Christian social thought between the wars. Yet the most

significant artifact of the twenties in terms of our topic was the Conference
on Christian Politics, Economics and Citizenship (the world had not yet
gone goofy on acronyms but the conference was known as Copec); and
Copec was definitely the product of ecumenical collaboration. The 1909
Matlock Conference of the Student Christian Movement, of which Temple
was chair, had quickened the social conscience of many Christians,
including the Congregationalist Malcolm Spencer.[62] He had been keenly
evangelical at Oxford but was also, atypically, interested in social issues,
partly under the tutelage of Scott Holland and Gore. At Matlock he
proposed that some sort of structure be established to extend the analytical
and prophetic work of the Conference. The result was the "Collegium,"
with Temple as chair and with Lucy Gardner, who played a central role at
Copec, as secretary.[63] It functioned as a discussion group and produced one
book, *Competition.*

The preliminary thinking having been done through the "Collegium," the
Copec   movement   was   officially   launched   in   1919   at   the
interdenominational Conference of Christian Social Unions, with Gore in
the chair. It was given strong support by the Lambeth Conference of the
following year. By 1923, 200,000 questionnaires were being processed by
seventy five centers around the country: the preparation for Copec was
massive.[64]

One of the non-Anglicans who figured prominently at Copec was S. E.
Keeble, a Methodist. Born in 1853, he had been active in the Christian
socialist revival of the eighties and nineties and had founded the Wesleyan
Methodist Union for Social Service. "The acknowledged leader of radical
thinkers within Methodism," Keeble was clearly to the left of the vast
majority of his co-religionists.[65] He argued for women's suffrage and for
state control of land, minerals and railroads. As were so many Anglicans,
Keeble was influenced by Edward Caird and T. H. Green. He was a
pacifist, a friend of the Soviet Union and of its apologist, Julius Hecker and
in close contact with American social gospel figures like Harry F. Ward of
Union Seminary. Keeble was in general agreement with the League of the
Kingdom of God, the Guild of St. Matthew and the Christian Social Union
and supported, although not uncritically, the Labour Party; Philip Snowden
attributed his conversion to socialism to reading Keeble's writings.[66]

Keeble represented a distinct minority view within Methodism but he was
heir to a tradition of social analysis the exemplar of which was Hugh Price
Hughes, who was born in Chartist times and died in 1902. Hughes, like
Keeble, was a proponent of Green's "ethics of altruism" and worked for
heightened awareness of the relevance of theology to social thought through

his "Forward Movement" and via the *Methodist Times*, of which he was the editor.   William McGuire King, in a June, 1984 *Journal of Religious History* article, viewed Hughes' work as an attempt to deal with impending cultural isolation, as urbanization and secularization took their toll on religious practice.   The intent was to "relieve the cultural stress upon Christianity" by widening the definition of religion to include concern for social structures.   To the many who had rejected the old individualistic piety, Hughes and others wanted to say "Take another look; the faith is still important, the church still worth belonging to."   Thus King underscored, as I do, the apologetical impulse behind Christian involvement in social issues. He wrongly, however, saw this involvement springing almost exclusively from a fearful, defensive attitude, failing to take into account the movement toward a more comprehensive theology symbolized by *Lux Mundi*. Christian social thought, in either its Anglican or Methodist forms, cannot be accounted for exclusively or even principally in terms of an indecorous race for relevance.[67]

Keeble's "greatest book,"[68] *Christian Responsibility for the Social Order*, came out in 1922 and displayed the depth of the tradition of Christian reflection on society to which both he and Hughes laid claim.   In it he demonstrated less of the boldness of the Fifth Report and more of the caution that would emerge at Copec two years later.   He began his presentation by conducting a conventional social Christian exegetical tour of the Bible: the prophets were the early preachers of social justice; Jesus, in their train, preached the immanence of the Kingdom of God and was himself known as Son of Man, a collective term; the Sermon on the Mount sets out ethical canons for a righteous society.   He was unusual, however, in his warning of the dangers of a millenarian position, which some wanted to derive from biblical apocalyptic.   An overemphasis on sudden catastrophe, Keeble argued, can cut the nerve of social passion and call into question the tractability present problems.[69]

He went on to rehearse social themes in the early Fathers...even Barnabas...citing the American social reformer W. D. P. Bliss.   He had many good things to say about the Middle Ages, as did many Anglicans in this period, as I have noted.   He thought the medievals were wise in regarding economics as a branch of theology, thereby placing it in the context of value.   Indeed, the fifteenth century was the "Golden Age of Labour." Moving to the nineteenth century, Keeble noted the influence of Methodism on Chartism and asserted that Christian socialism, which came out of that era, was affected by Continental thinkers like Fourier and St. Simon.[70]   The cooperative movement, which also got its start around mid-century, did so apart from social Christianity, Keeble argued.[71]

Turning to modern social Christianity, Keeble offered an analysis that differs little from material that can be found in numbers of books on the subject. He traced the movement back to Shelley, Wordsworth, Coleridge, Southey, Cowper and Blake, all, he wrote, Christians or at least Christian in their social sensibilities. Carlyle had enormous impact, notably through *Past and Present* and his disciple, Ruskin, both as aesthetic analyst and social philosopher, wielded wide influence. Ruskin and also, importantly, William Morris, decried the mechanization of work and life and the wast and injury to human character arising from fierce competition in trade.[72] Keeble was in the mainstream of social Christianity if not of Methodist thinking when he urged taking Ruskin and Morris seriously on a political level. And, while he realized that the righting of industrial wrongs would necessarily involve collective action, he also shared Belloc's fear of domination by an omnicompetent state. The "ruling principles" he put forward are reminiscent of Temple's thought but they are not yet sharpened into *media axiomata*: subordination of material to spiritual values; respect for personality; the ruling motive to be service, not profit-making; observance of "Christian social justice."

In general, Keeble's writing tends to be prolix and, in depth and in originality, is not up to the standards of his Anglican counterparts. It shows, however, that social Christianity knew no denominational barriers and that in Great Britain there was a common theological, literary and philosophical tradition upon which all could draw and a common universe of discourse in which all participated. Copec was the flower of that tradition in its time and in its speaking of the issues and, together with the organization that resulted from it, was a significant gift of ecumenical British Christianity to the world. Keeble's work along with that of others helped shape the context that made Copec both possible and, to the extent that it was, successful.

The year 1922 saw Lloyd-George, no longer able to keep the wartime coalition cobbled together, resign, to be succeeded by Bonar-Law; after the general election Baldwin became Chancellor of the Exchequer. The economy was beginning to slow down and, as a measure of thrift that presaged further and more drastic cuts in the ensuing years, fresh grants for housing schemes under the Addison Act were curtailed.[73] The celebrated Lord Northcliffe died, with his newspaper empire passing under the control of his brother, Lord Rothermere and, in the nascent broadcasting industry, the British Broadcasting Company (soon to become a corporation) was formed. This was also the year in which Tawney presented the substance of his 1926 landmark *Religion and the Rise of Capitalism* as the first Scott

Holland Memorial Lecture, a prestigious pulpit for social Christianity between the wars.[74]

Tawney's (and Weber's) pioneering work is well known and does not require recounting here. What I would like to highlight is Tawney's role as a Christian social critic. He was by profession an economic historian, the closest any interwar Christian thinker came to being involved professionally with the discipline of economics (the outstanding exception being Lord Stamp); and this lack of technical expertise was held up, validly, as a pronounced weakness in the movement by its detractors. His study of economic history was not done simply to account for change in the mercantile life of humankind in time and space. Rather, he was at pains, in his words, "to emphasize the instrumental character of economic activities by reference to an ideal which is held to express the true nature of man."[75] Anthropology, for Tawney, was fundamental. When it is lost sight of, the admirable enterprising spirit that produced much exhilaration and transformed the face of the material world decays into "the uncritical worship of economic power": economic efficiency becomes an end instead of a means.[76] As he had done in his earlier book *Equality*[77] Tawney attacked the "idolatry of wealth" that he saw in post-war Britain and called for a more equal distribution of the economy's bounty. Here Tawney stood squarely in the tradition of the Fifth Report and his prophetic stance would be mirrored by Christian thinkers throughout the period.

More than a few of those thinkers were to turn to the Middle Ages for models of the ideal social order but Tawney was not to join their essentially fruitless quest. True, he was quite willing to praise the medievals' honesty in calling sin, sin: for them, greed was not "enterprise" nor avarice, "economy." And he valued highly their synthesis of the external order and the religion of the spirit in which the disparate parts are related to a single end.[78] Yet he argued against a romantic, homogeneous view of the Middle Ages that fails to recognize that "there is a medieval Puritanism and rationalism as well as[79] a medieval Catholicism."[80] Tawney, who was active in Labour Party politics and served on the Hadow and Sankey Commissions, was less interested in casting society in the image of an "ideal type" than in taking practical steps toward extending the democratic idea into new spheres. Thus he was able to merge his theologically-based convictions about healthy human community with the profoundly ethical strain in "secular" English socialism, referred to in the previous chapter, to become what W. H. Greenleaf calls the most influential Christian social thinker of his time.

In the same year (1922) as Tawney's Scott Holland Lectures, a book was published by a group of churchmen deeply imbued with the spirit of the Middle Ages. *The Return of Christendom* was shaped by members of a small study group convened by the Rev. P. E. T. Widdrington. Widdrington had been a friend of Ramsay MacDonald at Oxford (he seems to have been in love with Enid Stacy, a feminist and Fabian, whom Widdrington later married) and was early drawn to the Labour cause. He had served as curate, with Conrad Noel, under the socialist W. E. Moll and was an active member of the Church Socialist League, which reached its peak in 1921. Already in 1919, he had brought together an informal group of clerical and lay members of the Church of England at Paycocke's House, Coggeshall, at the first meeting of which the topic was "Church and People in the Middle Ages."[81] These discussion sessions at Paycocke's resulted in the formation of the League of the Kingdom of God, out of the old CSL and, beginning in 1925, the Anglo-Catholic Summer School of Sociology at Keble College, Oxford.

Widdrington worked closely with a wealthy layman, Maurice Reckitt (mustard and laundry products), editor of the *Church Socialist* from 1915 to 1919. In his autobiography Reckitt writes that the publication of *The Return of Christendom* was premature: it had no chapter on international order, its theology was insufficiently harmonized and its social thinking tentative.[82] Nevertheless, it was a widely read commercial success and contained the main lines of thought that would be pursued at the Summer Schools and through the pages of *Christendom*, founded in 1931. The various authors drove home the point that, in the absence of a body of distinctly Christian social thought, the field was abandoned to purely secular programs. What was needed was a recovery of the idea that the Kingdom of God is a Divine Order which, when expressed in temporal political forms, creates a climate conducive to the exercise of Christian virtue. The medieval synthesis was by no means accepted wholesale but already in *Return* it is lifted up as the best available model for post-war society that had lost its bearings. In this single, universal community, governed by God, economics would be a subset of ethics, labor would be held in high esteem, property would be regarded as an extension of personality and as a means of service and prices, controlled by the government, would be just, not exploitive.[83] It was this expansive, catholic vision that the Paycocke's group labored long to recover and to apply to a society in serious trouble and I will return to their work in the next chapter, on the 1930's, in which it came to full expression. In the 1920', only the first steps were being taken along the road toward an organic Christian theology of the social order.

That road was being paved most noticeably, in the early twenties, by the

Anglo-Catholic party in the Church of England. At a time when evangelicals, both inside and outside the national church, still soaked in the spirit of liberal individualism, were concerned with issues of conversion and personal piety; when the Modernists were preoccupied with doctrine and the church at large was concerned with the ministries of women, temperance and Prayer Book revision,[84] people of the High Church persuasion were paying major attention to the ills and to the promise of post-war society, particularly from the point of view of its least-favored members.

This may come as something of a surprise to anyone familiar with the social gospel movement in America. Here, social passion tended to be fostered in liberal Protestant circles, not in confessional and liturgical contexts. It participated in the spirit of activist pragmatism, carrying, as it moved, light theological luggage.[85] It worked closely with the labor movement and thus had some basis in the working class, which was never the case for social Christianity in Great Britain. It tended to hold a "low" view of the church, regarding it instrumentally, as a means to the end of social betterment, rather than as the "divine society" of Tractarian emphasis.

What, then, accounts for the urge toward social righteousness that moved through Anglo-Catholic ranks? I think there are a number of necessary, although not sufficient causes that can be posited. There is, first, the Maurician tradition, which spoke to Christians who took dogmas seriously of divine intrusion into human life, of an Incarnation intensive in Christ and extensive in the material world. In this *locus* alone, Anglo-Catholics had a base from which to attack the idealist separation of spirit and matter that underlay privatized forms of faith. These "materialist" and "immanentist" accents blended well with a robust and earthy catholic sacramentalism that viewed God as hallowing all of creation, forming a universal community in Baptism, nourishing a common life of fellowship and service in the Eucharist. What liberal Protestants derived from nineteenth century liberal theology...the Father hood of God, the Brotherhood of Man...Anglo-Catholics were able to derive directly from the classical creeds and dogmas of the church. For them, both a social critique and a social vision were latent in the *depositum fidei*.

The critique of industrial society by way of Carlyle, Ruskin and Morris, a critique at once aesthetic and ethical, enjoyed a high profile in English intellectual life and reinforced the thrust toward change, given impetus by the post-war situation and by the preaching of the Kingdom of God. Strengthening this critical tradition and in part arising from it was a popular medievalism which, when it was not frittering away its time dreaming about

Scottian castles and Wordsworthian villages, could provide images of what we might now call a holistic social life, the elements of which are integrated, related to each other in a single quest for the Good, True and Beautiful. A final cause was the perception, common among Christians after the war, that secular culture was unable to offer a way out of its own destruction; in this situation, Anglo-Catholicism was ideally positioned to offer possibilities: its historic business had been the preservation and promotion of timeless Christian doctrine, of a moral code and the axioms of a just social order apposite to all people in all times. This confidence in its sources, coupled with "the belief in the possibility of social reform by conscious effort"[86] gave the Anglo-Catholic movements for social reform at once a stability and boldness unmatched between the wars.

The first Anglo-Catholic Congress, successor to the English Church Union founded in 1859, was held in 1920 and concerned itself, *inter alia*, with social themes. Prominent on the program was a speech by L. S. Thornton, a member of Charles Gore's Community of the Resurrection in the industrial town of Mirfield, on the Kingdom of God. The church, he said, is the primary embodiment of the Kingdom but is not an end in itself; it is the "indispensable organ" of the Kingdom, the influence of which is "percolating in society." Thornton, unlike many of his colleagues, had no truck with medieval Christendom. "We are naturally attracted by medieval Christendom," he admitted, "a theocracy in which human society is transplanted bodily into the Church and subsumed under its categories."[87] The times, however, are different and the church must generate criticism of the "world," i.e., society organized apart from the law of God, on a variety of fronts. A single focus will not be adequate. Yet the modern world itself is locked into a single focus. "Deprived of imagination by the pursuit of material things, [moderns] inevitably rest in the temporary security of some system which is ready to hand and looks inevitable."[88] The Protest legacy of religion as personal piety is impotent in the face of this enervating fatalism. Only a strong catholicism, proclaimed Thornton, has the resources for "criticising or consecrating the organization of our common life." And in the midst of persuading Congress participants, many of whom needed persuading, of the necessity of an "interfering" Christianity, he introduced the apologetic theme never absent from Christian social thinking: the church will enhance its attraction if it can convince people that "the great iron world of necessity, in which they earn their bread, can be made to bow before the sovereignty of God."[89] As to precisely how that genuflection was to be effected, Thornton offered no hint.

Well on his way to becoming the patriarch of social Christianity in Great

Britain, Charles Gore appeared at the Congress to second Thornton's appeal for sustained religious reflection on the social order. The primitive church, he said, made an impact because of its moral life, not because of its doctrine or order. In it, the rich got poorer, the poor became better off and everyone was provided for by right, not as a result of subjective charitable impulses. This sense of moral pioneering needs to be recovered in our own day, Gore said. But it will be difficult to come by because the Roman Church "offers salvation on easy terms" and the Church of England is too busy being the *national* church, tending to equate moral duty with obeying the civil laws. Such a church, he said, would have little to say, prophetically, to a society that placed a higher value on property than on people (a recurring social Christian theme). The solution? "Let us have fewer Christians if so be, but better."[90] Gore was also concerned at the Congress with personal moral issues: the church must stand for Christian marriage, he argued, and against "sinful" conception control. On the latter, he was outside the mainstream, as the church came rather quickly to place family planning in the context of responsible private choice.

If Thornton was cautious about wholesale adoption of the medieval model, another Congress guest, Gilbert Keith Chesterton, was not. The Middle Ages, he proclaimed, had "more of liberty than socialism, more of equality than capitalism, and more fraternity than either."[91] The modern world is the result of the disintegration of the medieval synthesis, with an anti-Christian spirit in the ascendency, a spirit that promotes skepticism, rationalism and worldliness. Yet Chesterton, like Thornton, suggested no program for social renovation, being content with the observation that "it is necessary to insist that it was in the very best period of Christian rule, in the Middle Ages, when the whole of the Catholic spirit and system were present, that the best attempt at a social solution was made.[92] Disputable history indeed! (See footnote number 83).

Christian social thinkers were much in evidence at the 1923 Congress, at which 1,976 priests and 12,926 laypeople jammed the Albert Hall and £27,000 was collected for missions. K. E. Kirk, Henry Slesser, W. H. Frere, Mary Scharlieb, M. D., Studdert Kennedy and Gore were joined by the American Episcopal social gospel advocate J. O. S. Huntington and by Francis J. Hall of General Seminary, New York. Also present was Frank Weston, the enormously popular Bishop of Zanzibar, who electrified the Congress in a speech urging what today might be called a preferential option for the poor. "You cannot claim to worship Jesus in the Tabernacle," he thundered, "if you do not pity Jesus in the slum." This sentence quickly assumed canonical authority among Anglo-Catholics and was quoted again and again in the interwar years. For many, it was a summons to the moral reconstruction of the social system. For others, it highlighted the old model of the slum parish and its charitable work among the urban poor. And this may have been more coincidental with Weston's own cast of mind. "I know nothing of politics or economics," he said the same year.[93]

The introduction to the report of the 1923 Congress, by Francis Underhill and Charles Scott Gillett, underscored the need for Weston's admonition. Anglo-Catholicism, they admitted, had a tendency to deteriorate into a "pious clique," unengaged with the world. Yet its message has definite social implications: all are equal, all labor is hallowed, the material world is the locus of divine activity. The problem has been that voices raised in prophetic protests against an anti-human social order have not gone on to teach; what is needed now is a "newly formulated apologetic" that will relate Christ and society in useful ways.

Attempts were made to rise to this challenge by several Congress speakers. Henry Slesser, an attorney, praised the medieval idea of the Mass at the center of community life, then went on to argue, curiously, that when faith in the real presence began to decline, money became the central inspiration.[94] Another speaker, John Lee, pointed to the leavening effect religion had in medieval times because it was taken seriously, then went on to advance the murky thought that the task ahead was not to restore the society of the Middle Ages but to "realize the ideal." The Middle Ages also appealed to Studdert Kennedy. In that period, he said, the purpose of ritual was to consecrate all of life, including the communal aspects, to God. Yet in modern Britain, he lamented, "I have been to Mass in churches where I felt it was sinful, sinful because there was no passion for social righteousness behind it."[95] And it was the case that, despite the high profile maintained by prominent social thinkers in the church, many remained convinced that "Christian socialism" was an oxymoron.[96]

In the early twenties, Hewlett Johnson was emerging on the scene as a forceful spokesperson for the Christian left, a role he played throughout the interwar years and on into the post-war period (he died in 1966). Johnson was not an Anglo-Catholic, although he "learned much of the high church movement on its happier side" from his friend, Canon Lewis Donaldson, leader of the legendary Leicester-to-Westminster workers' march.[97] One of a number of horses he was beginning to ride was the Social Credit scheme of Major C. H. Douglas, a system aiming a equalizing the availability of credit but based on economic fallacies refutable by any tyro student of the subject.[98] Although Temple was characteristically cautious, stopping short of embracing Douglas while complimenting Orage's *The New Age* for calling attention to the manipulation of credit,[99] Johnson, also characteristically, became an outright Douglasite. In an April, 1922 article in *The Pilgrim*, he admitted his attraction to Douglas was based to some extent on their shared backgrounds as engineers. The special attraction of social credit, Johnson wrote, was that, if adopted, it would attain the medieval ideal of the Just Price "in a thoroughly scientific manner." He was to continue his advocacy of the scheme throughout the interwar period, maintaining its efficacy long after its influence, which for a time was considerable, had waned.[100]

The Pilgrim's concerns were extremely broad-ranging, from the new science of psychology to international affairs. Editorially, it supported the League of Nations, the shrine at which nearly everyone was paying homage in the twenties, but criticized it for lacking the power of sanction. The journal was favorably inclined toward Lloyd-George but still approved of the result of the general election of November, 1922, which installed a comfortable Conservative majority in Parliament and Andrew Bonar Law in the Prime Minister's office. The former warring nations, it observed, were still belligerent and only exhaustion prevents them from going to war. Russia, a "hideous nightmare," has betrayed the lofty ideals that originally inspired its revolution (Britain recognized Soviet Russia in 1924). Hewlett Johnson, on the other hand, was to carry on a lifelong *apologia* for the revolution, unable to adjust his thinking even when the Stalinist purges came to light.

In the spring of 1923, Temple outlined for his readers his "Big Four" Christian social principles: (1) *Liberty*, respect for each person by everyone, deriving from a common humanity under one divine Father; (2) *Fellowship*; (3) *The Duty of Service*, the assumption of one's proper vocation; (4) *The Power of Sacrifice*, the spiritual value of the voluntary suffering of the innocent.[101] He also wrote of the large body of agreement that he saw among socially sensitive Christians, an observation that was correct as far as broad moral impulses and general social *desiderata* were concerned, and voiced the confidence that this consensual corpus would become better known in the church through the upcoming Copec meeting. It was to be seen as the Everest event, not only of 1924 but of the entire period between the wars.

Yet where Temple, as was his wont, saw a great deal of unanimity in the church regarding its attitude toward the social order, Gilbert Clive Binyon found confusion. In 1924 he outlined five possible ideas associated with the phrase "Christian Socialism": (1) Christian principles are to be applied to all of life, including mercantile and political area; (2) Concerted, practical efforts should be directed toward eradicating evils such as sweat shops and slums; (3) The church preaching the ideal of wide distribution of property, encouraging individual crafts and a non-factory, family-based production unit; (4) Co-operative societies of producers or self-governing workshops; (5) The regular Labour and Socialist programs.[102]

For his own part, Binyon ruled the first notion out of court: it does not focus on the necessary structural changes. The second he regarded as non-theoretical if, nevertheless, honorable and needed. The Fourth idea is a phase of the third. Therefore, what was left was a choice among three meanings of Christian Socialism: a practical Christianity, socially reformist but non-ideological; distributism or socialism. Having already eliminated the first, he was confronted with collectivist and on-collectivist options. Binyon remained on the horns of this dilemma, embracing neither completely and thereby reflecting the traditional chariness within the church of identifying the Kingdom with a secular ideology or of making the boundaries of Christian social concern and those of the Labour Party's agenda simply coextensive.   He was very clear, however, on the apologetical urgency surrounding the church's search for a social theology. He thought it should try to make its message appealing in twin directions: toward socialists who aren't Christian and toward Christians who aren't socialists.   He was not sure how a "Christian Sociology" would differ materially both from distributism and from socialism, although by 1931 he seems to have moved closer to an "autochthonous" view; and already in 1924 Binyon was quite sure that a successful discovery of such a sociology was the only way toward presenting the Christian case winsomely to a wider public.[103]

To reach a wider public with the churches' message of social righteousness and, indeed, to discuss precisely what principles and proposals might be implicated in that message, were the goals of the Conference on Christian Politics, Economics and Citizenship held in Birmingham in April, 1924. It was an extraordinary gathering. Delegates numbered 1,500, eighty of whom came from outside the British Isles. Messages were presented from the King, from Prime Minister Ramsay MacDonald, who had only recently assumed office in the first Labour Government[104] and from Baldwin and Asquith. The tone of the conference was confident; the enveloping dismay, characteristic of the years after the Crash, had not yet descended on the country. The mood was caught and in a large degree set by the chair, Temple, in sentences like this one, from his opening address: "With the steadily growing sense that Machiavellian statecraft is bankrupt there is an increasing readiness to give heed to the claims of Jesus Christ that He is the Way, the Truth and the Life."[105]

The work of the conference consisted in reading and discussion the reports of the twelve previously appointed commissions, the first and what Roger Lloyd calls the ablest, however, "The Nature of God and His Purpose for the World," never being considered.[106] Presumably, it was felt that, much in the spirit of the "Doctrine Divides, Service Unites" slogan of the later Life and Work committee, it was important to move rapidly to practical ways in which Christians could effect the Christianizing of the social order. The intense search for theoretical models would be a feature of the next decade, after the "Years of Gold" (A. J. P. Taylor) failed to produce the thorough reconstruction of society for which many had hoped.

What Copec produced, according to its chair, was, in the first instance, not political, practical or ideological but spiritual, a feeling of unity in the service of one Lord. And more than one observer commented on the sincere moral tone evident throughout the week as well as on Temple's deft chairing. Yet the conference was not without consequences and Temple, looking back seventeen years later, listed three: 1) reform of the penal system was advanced; 2) a vast extension of secondary education took place; 3) the housing situation improved considerably.[107] It also produced a report, *Politics and Citizenship* which, while in the Fifth Report tradition, was more conservative than its predecessor, urging that the church be concerned only with ultimate ends, not with proximate means.[108] Several years after the conference, under the direction of the Copec Central Committee and Advisory Council, a series of twelve pamphlets was issued, written by a number of prominent thinkers, not all of them Christians, including Gore, Temple, Studdert Kennedy, A. D. Lindsay, J. R. Benn, Harold Laski, William Paton and H. G. Wood. Nor was Copec without institutional effect. In addition to the Central Committee, a continuation conference was formed in Newcastle which became, in 1925, the Bureau of Social Research for Tynside, directed by H. A. Mess. It issued, in 1928, an investigative report, *Industrial Tynside*, which helped to raise the level of awareness about the growing unemployment problem in the decaying smokestack industries.

The Copec structure was officially dismantled in January, 1929 with the formation of the ecumenical Council of Christian Churches for Social Questions (CSC). It was composed of seventy-two members, thirty from the national church and did its work with five committees: international, youth, local cooperation, social education and research. Its Director of Research until 1933 was the brilliant V. A. Demant, about whom I will have more to say below. The research work of the CSC was financed by the Halley Stewart Trust.[109]

Copec's ecumenical impact was not limited to Great Britain. Its reports constituted the British contribution to the 1925 Stockholm Life and Work Conference, with the subsequent work of which both non-Anglican Alfred Garvie and Temple would be heavily involved. Indeed, the whole movement was launched from a solid cooperative base. As Edward Shillito pointed out at the time, Copec stood in debt to the foundational work done by the Roman Catholic Fr. Charles Plater and was in succession to the 1911 Swanwick Social Service Union conferences begun the following year.[110] S. E. Keeble styled it a "social Edinburgh," referring to the great missionary conference of 1910.[111]

Reacting to Copec, Maurice Reckitt rendered the judgment that the period after the conference was "something of an anti-climax," although this reflects his perhaps inflated hopes for an emerging sociology more than it does Copec's real achievements.[112] In a similar vein and from a similar bias, Philip Mairet, writing in 1956, opined that Copec led to very little. This overly-harsh evaluation Mairet based on the fact that it did not come up with "a practical political agenda, such as could be submitted to a Government."[113]   As could be expected, archcritic Herbert Hensley Henson's attitude was dismissive in *Quo Tendimus?* (1924) and summarized in his autobiography thus: "The sentimental-socialist version of Christianity has its Vatican in S. Martin's and its Nicaea at Copec. Dick Sheppard [of St. Martin's-in-the-Fields] is its prophet and Temple has hitherto been its pope."[114]   Copec erred, he thought, in attempting to impose a united Christian will on society and he regarded the conference as an example of the currently fashionable "secularized conception of Christianity."

Others were kinder. W. M. Pryke, writing in *Modern Churchman*, a journal normally uninterested in social matters, was highly critical of Henson's comments and praised the work of Copec, especially in the area of education.[115] A foreign observer, who had been present in Birmingham, theologian Justus F. Laun, felt that the conference had been successful in at least two respects: it combined the ecumenical impulse with the current vision of social reconstruction and it deduced a social gospel, not from secular tenets, but from fundamental Christian principles. He traced part of the Copec lineage back to John Brown Paton, a Congregationalist, and his work in the 1880s with the High Anglican Earl Nelson and, interestingly, from the point of view of this presentation, saw suggestions of it in *Lux Mundi*.[116] Reviewer E. Lyttleton, in *Theology*, thought that the conference brought nearer "an era of progress and quickened hope" but he looked askance at church folk joining hands with, on the one hand, Christians of other denominations and, on the other, with pagans for social progress. He cautioned that religion must be integral and not ancillary to reform, with the church's main duty, however, being to "rouse the conscience."[117]

Copec was, of course, discussed in Canterbury Convocation. The Bishop of Winchester recalled the efforts of small groups that led up to Birmingham. Although they had some influence, "they had been regarded in many quarters if not as faddists, at any rate as idealists and visionaries, and even the Report of the Archbishop's Committee was viewed with grave dislike and suspicion."[118] The Bishop saw Copec marking a turning point, after which it becomes imperative that the church pay much more attention to economic and social issues. A larger effort must go into "making democracy safe for the world," including strong church support for the League of Nations. Indiscretions and exaggerations there were, said Winchester, but Copec was a movement of the Spirit nevertheless and the Bishop's warm reception of the conference was generally shared by his colleagues.

The Pilgrim, which ran a complete report on Copec in its October, 1924 issue, had offered a perceptive article the previous July by N. E. Edgerton Swann, associated with the League of the Kingdom of God, which held its first Summer School that summer. Titled "The Fallacy of Latinism," it was a very sober, balanced analysis of what its author saw as his age's desperate quest for coherence and certitude. That quest, he said, was leading many back to the Middle Ages and even those who don't idealize the period see some good in it and observe its useful values being eroded in contemporary culture. Edgerton Swann warned, however, that this search for the whole and steady view could degenerate into "belligerent partisanship" of the sort represented by Belloc's *Europe and Faith*.[119] This tendency, the Latinism of his title, was characterized by sectarianism and provincialism. That belligerent partisanship became a feature of the thirties is a testimony both to Edgerton Swann's prescience and to the increasing desperation of the quest.

"Latinism" found friendly lodgement in the early twenties, as I have mentioned, within Anglo-Catholicism. On the strength of the latter's waxing strength, the *Green Quarterly* was inaugurated in January, 1924 and its initial issue carried an article by the prolific Henry Slesser on "The Social Implications of the Catholic Faith." Slesser, who served as Solicitor General in the first Labour government, thought that there was "everything to admire" in the medieval conception of a Holy Empire and was a leading advocate of "return to Christendom" ideas in the church.[120]

The most dreamily romantic, as well as one of the most gifted and eccentric figures in the medievalism movement was Arthur J. Penty. His 1923 book *Toward a Christian Sociology* was a ringing call to a Christian "social gospel" based on the absolute standards of the Kingdom of God. And already in this most mellow and prosperous period in the interwar years, he talked the language of disaster, the avoidance of which lay in a "return to simpler conditions of life and society," meaning, for Penty, a decentralized, anti-industrial ruralism.[121] In typical social Christian style he derided dualistic theologies that split spirit from matter and included in this regard a fine critique of Augustine, whom Christian social thinkers tended to ignore. Penty was not consistent, however, and elsewhere seemed to favor spirit over matter, especially as the latter takes highly evolved technological form. He was also hopelessly unrealistic about power and politics, falling into the intellectualistic trap of assuming that change would occur almost automatically, if only doctrine got squared away and people thought rightly. Penty was only the most egregious example of this type of political naivete; a rarefied intellectualism was to plague Christian social thought and compromise its effectiveness throughout the twenties and thirties.

Hardly non-political, by contrast, was A. Maude Royden, prominently represented in a series of occasional papers issued by *The Church Militant*, beginning in February, 1924 with a piece on "The Dock Strike" and continuing through 1927. Labor in agriculture and on the docks is the most oppressed, she declared. In protesting their oppression, they may lack middle class decorum, but society should not sniff: it is society that has tolerated the conditions which evoke rough response. She evinced no idealized view of the working class...she pointed out that she had once lived in Poplar and knew whereof she spoke...but praised its members' real virtues as she called for fair treatment for them. This attitude was typical of social Christian thinkers in general, as was Royden's refusal to offer specific remedies beyond the encouragement of enlightened public opinion. Royden was also concerned, in 1924, with capital punishment, which she opposed and with housing.[122] The following year saw the publication of a pamphlet on arbitration, a "buzzword" of the era. Along with many others, she was concerned that the League of Nations had no power to enforce its policies; all nations, she thought, should join the twenty three smaller states in pledging to submit all disputes to binding arbitration by the Permanent Court of International Justice. Farsighted, she saw a large-scale war on the way. She suggested that "if Europe proceeds along the path of war America will be drawn in too-for what is the Atlantic to a modern aerial fleet?"[123]

Some observers of social Christianity between the wars are inclined to emphasize its weakness, its lack of impact and its theoretical confusion. The fact remains, however, that no group "won" the battle for the heart and soul of post-World War II Britain; radical socialism was not installed nor did the old liberalism triumph. Rather, a consensus gradually developed about the reconstruction of the social order that was an amalgam of traditions. One cannot fault social Christianity for failing to erect the *respublica Christiana* in the green and pleasant land, although one can fault its partisans for their failure to strive for a more univocal voice. Nor can they be condemned outright for beating a retreat, as they did in the twenties, away from "political perplexities" to "higher theological ground."[124] No one was exempt in this "decade of dismay" from the challenge to set his or her theoretical house in order and social Christian thinkers, if they did not rise above the standards of their era, in the main did not fall below them.

I offer as an example another series of topical pamphlets, issued by the old socialist Clarion Press in 1924. They sold for a penny and were called "Pass on Pamphlets," the idea being that the purchaser, having read, marked, learned and inwardly digested the contents, would make it available to other readers. The quality of these pamphlets was in no way superior to that of their religious counterparts.

Everything that keeps women in their (subservient) place, trumpeted Julia Dawson in "Why Women Want Socialism," will disappear when the latter becomes reality. Financial worries, bad housing, even war will be fossils. How wonderful it will be for the distaff side when, under socialism, "experts will come into our homes to do the cleaning regularly," with the laundry and cooking being done, somehow, on a public basis! Yet the hard political and social issues were not addressed by Dawson and the argument shaded into silliness.

If Dawson had some new ideas about domestic arrangements, the Clarion folks had nothing novel to offer about religion from the standpoint of secular socialism, managing only to come up with a reprint of a late-Victorian piece on "The New Religion" by the famous Robert Blatchford. A long-time propagandist for the fashionable religious iconoclasm of his times, the author waxed euphoric, in prose tending to shades of light violet, about a humanistic faith reminiscent of Comte and emphasizing love, liberty, holiness and the beauty of life. People "endowed with spirit," he said, could not grow in the horrible industrial towns, "so our religion bans them." For other religious views, the Clarion pamphleteers had to reach beyond their strictly secular ranks. George Lansbury, who wrote a tract in the same year, "Jesus and Labour" for the Labour Party, was recruited to pen "Socialism for the Poor." Conrad Noel, too, contributed "Socialism and Church Tradition," written some years earlier when he was organizing for the quite political Church Socialist League. For Noel, Christian involvement with socialism was not a cheap ploy designed for evangelistic purposes: "the Socialist account of Christ's religion is the one true interpretation which all Christians are bound to accept." Still, he warned that if the church did not *carpe diem* and promote socialism, God would take away the Kingdom and give it to secularists bringing forth the fruit thereof. The intellectual fruit, however, was no better in the secular orchards than it was in the sacred groves.

There was organizational as well as cerebral activity going on in these years. In 1923 (or 1924)[125] the Church Socialist League, which had a collectivist bent, disbanded. Those members, like Widdrington, Reckitt and Demant, who favored the construction of a theologically-based Christian sociology, founded the League of the Kingdom of God. It ran the Summer School of Sociology, already mentioned; at this stage it displayed a bias against collectivism and was skeptical of the League of Nations. T. C. Gobat, pacifist and veteran Anglo-Catholic socialist, served as chair, with Reckitt as secretary and Widdrington as national organizer.[126] Henry Slesser played a leading role. In 1924, loyal CSL socialists joined with non-Anglican Christians to form the Society for Socialist Christians (which is sometimes mistakenly referred to in the literature as the Society of Christian Socialists). Fred Hughes was its chair and Charles Record its secretary. It combined elements of the old Socialist Quaker Society and the Free Church Socialist League and it also admitted non-Christians to membership. R. H. Tawney was a member at a later stage.[127] In 1931, after a Christian Socialist Crusade led by a group of MPs, the SCS became the Socialist Christian League.

One of the issues that divided social Christians, inside and outside the "little societies," was how far individuals and groups should become involved in partisan politics. For some, the Labour Party platform summarized their ethical democratic socialism; for others, politics was taboo, with only the private, agapeistic route open. What was hardly ever discussed, however, was the prospect of a Christian parliamentary party on the Continental model. In one of the few references to the subject I was able to find, Maurice Reckitt dismissed it in a few sentences. Correctly, he pointed out that there was an insufficient theological and philosophical background available upon which to erect a religious party. He also noted that Continental Christians parties often disagreed strongly among themselves on political, not theological points. And in Great Britain, socially-minded people in the churches lacked the unity of principle and purpose which was a requisite for initiating a political movement. What about Christians forming a caucus within one or another of the existing parties? Reckitt thought this strategy was bound for shipwreck on the shoals of the question of party loyalty: on crucial votes, would a Christian leader urge his bloc to vote contrary to the party's line?[128]

I would add that no one saw any room on the political spectrum for another party, nor was there any reason to believe that a new party, even if it shouldered its way onto the spectrum, had any chance of succeeding (note, e.g., the fate of Mosley's New Party). Also, the majority of church people were not converted to social readings of Christianity in the first place; of those that were, many were leery of associating the faith's principles and passions with specific legislation, while others attached great hope to the Labour Party and to the unions. For the emergence of a Christian political party, the unanimity, the momentum, the numbers and the opportunity were all lacking.

If there was little effort invested in direct political action, there were plenty of problems to address in these years of reconstruction, of "innovation, freedom and skepticism." One area of potential difficulty for society, that of race relations, was not given large attention at any time during the period. Indeed, what John Oliver calls the definitive study was already available by 1924, J. H. Oldham's *Christianity and the Race Problem*. By 1933 it had gone through nine editions.[129] Oldham's' basic premise was that we live in a shrinking world, the product of rapid technological advance, yet there has not been a corresponding moral advance. There is still too much talk of white supremacy, he thought, citing, *inter alia*, Lothrop Stoddard (*The Rising Tide of Colour*) and the American C. C. Josey, virtually an apologist for the Klan.[130] He then laid out a theological basis for the church's approach to this shrinking world in which contacts between the races were fast increasing. All are equal under the reign of God identified as Love, Oldham argued. Each person is of unique worth and the love of God should motivate each to serve the other. In developing the theological section Oldham made much use of Friedrich Von Hügel; his influence in general on his era was massive, yet he was typically not quoted, or was quoted infrequently, by interwar Christian social thinkers. (The Baron died in 1925).

Oldham discussed the causes of racial antagonism...the word "racism" had not yet come into vogue...ranging with a sure hand over the psychological, sociological and political data. He grasped cl early the importance of the study of heredity in the biological sciences, although he was not absolutely sure that acquired characteristics could not be genetically transmitted. Races differ in native capacity, he thought, but how and to what extent was not known. In fact, he came close to views popularized a few years ago by the American William Shockley, yet just at the point where he was about to shock modern sensibilities, he drew back into cautious vagueness.[131] Caution is the watchword of the book; it is forward-looking, especially in Oldham's extensive treatment of the problems of immigration, but not ringingly prophetic. Somewhat thin on theology, his discussion was nevertheless sensitive and probing and clearly ahead of its time.

Also less than theologically robust and touching on many of the same points as Oldham had the previous year was Basil Mathews' 1925 contribution *The Clash of Colour*. His plea was for a global rather than a nationalistic outlook and in this connection he urged attention to the growing importance of the Pacific basin. Breaking down racial barriers, he wrote, is the key to eliminating war and poverty.[132]

Thinkers in the twenties and thirties were attempting to "bake the big world all again" (Chesterton) and they but dimly perceived how profoundly British society would be affected by the villagizing of the globe and of the Empire and by the unprecedented influx of people from former colonies into England. Indeed, hindsight allows us to see how in many instances, especially that of the League of the Kingdom of God, the issue of pluralism was never adequately faced. The churches' response to the "race problem" is a case in point.[133]

With the splitting of the CSL was brought to an end what Binyon calls "the confusion of 1910-1924."[134] The confusion was over the direction in which the social movement in the church was to go, the "political" or the "theological" route. The key figure from the old days, Stewart Headlam, died in 1924. He had been instrumental in drawing together the sacramentalism of the Oxford Movement ritualists and the social concern of Maurice. Yet whereas Headlam had been politically inclined, after him the dominant force in Christian social thought was to be the neo-Thomism of the Christendom Group, whose central concern was to dissipate the confusion of the age, and of the church's thinking, by constructing an "autochthonous" religious approach to the social order.[135] Groups such as the Catholic Crusade would continue to exhibit more leftist and laborite colorations. But if social Christianity itself was viewed by many as marginal, these activist societies were seen as doubly so.

There was no question that various reforms of the social system were

going to be accomplished.[136] It was also clear, especially after the General
Strike, that they would not be accomplished by violence or along ideological
lines. The mood of the twenties, a mood that favored the introspective,
search-for-coherence stance of many Christian thinkers, was characterized
by a desire for "reconstruction, restoration and recovery." [137] It was a time
congenial to the beginning of the Anglo-Catholic Summer School of
Sociology and of the Social and Industrial Commission of the Church
Assembly, both of which occurred in 1925.

Not that all was completely quiet. The second Baldwin government,
convinced that unemployment woes were only temporary and that private
enterprise was the key to economic growth, returned the country to the gold
standard.[138] The results were not happy. There was increased labor unrest,
leading to "Red Friday," when the Triple Alliance threatened an embargo
on local transport if miners' wages were cut. The government averted the
embargo with a nine-month subsidy and bought more time by appointing
the Samuel Commission. Temple, who generally supported Baldwin,
thought that in this episode, the nation had "walked up to the very verge of
a precipice."[139] It was a foretaste of harsher trips to come.

Commenting on the international scene, Temple noted in April, 1925 that
there was tranquility but no real peace, with a great deal of fear abroad. Yet
when the Treaty of Locarno was signed in London in December he regarded
it as "one of the great steps forward in the direction of universal peace."[140]
Tawney agreed with Temple's assessment of the fear factor and looked with
stout hope to the League of Nations to relieve the tension. Economic
problems at home were caused, he thought, by the imposition of a hard
reparations policy, a policy which was backed, incorrectly, he reckoned, by
a working class that was suffering. He predicted, however, also mistakenly,
that strikes would continue to be confined to particular industries; a general
strike was deemed "not congenial to the traditions or temper of the British
Labour Movement."[141]

"Not a penny off the pay, not a minute on the day" was the slogan of the
miners in the General Strike that came in May, 1926. Their militancy was
deeply rooted in the injustices which they felt had been imposed on them by
the mine owners, whose hand was emboldened by the Samuel
Commission's argument that the wages subsidy had been a mistake. And
although feelings ran high on both sides, the Strike was an aberration and
in this light Tawney's prediction had been quite reasonable. As Keith
Middlemass points out, the triumph of the British political system in the
twentieth century has been the marriage between stability and change.
During the War, the state had learned to be a manager or mediator between

organized employers and organized labor. What evolved was a system
bound together by informality and representation, thus, among other effects,
granting church spokespersons access to the process. The state had a vested
interest, therefore, in supporting trade union leaders as they contended with
radicals on the fringes. One element of the system that was still flawed in
the twenties, contends Middlemass, was crisis management. The channels
of communication were still more open between government and business
than between government and labor. Thus, although the ideal was balance,
the scales were tipped in favor of the owners. The sound and fury of the
Strike, when it was over, signified almost no gain for labor.[142]

The Archbishop of Canterbury played an active role in trying to bring
about a settlement to the dispute.   Also active was the Bishop of
Manchester. Temple joined an *ad hoc* committee, convened by P. T. R.
Kirk of the Industrial Christian Fellowship to help find a compromise that
would bring the trouble to an ad end. The committee's work was a failure
and, some observers felt at the time, actually prolonged the miners' walkout
that persisted for six months after the ten-day General Strike. Seebohm
Rountree, e.g., argued that the miners hardened their position when they
imagined, inaccurately, that the churches were totally behind them. Later,
Temple admitted that it had been a botched affair but strongly defended
nevertheless the principle of Christian intervention in the name of
reconciliation.[143]

The Anglo-Catholic *Green Quarterly* declined to analyze the Strike in any
depth, remarking only and somewhat rosily on the good spirit displayed by
both sides. The Church of England, it thought, emerged with an ad
enhanced reputation.[144] Writing from the conservative side, A. C. Headlam
lambasted the Bishops, labeling their and the ICF's efforts "disastrous."
Echoing Cunningham, he reminded the meddlers that they should have had
more respect for iron economic laws, brute facts which make government
subsidies ineffectual. The churches' present duty is to condemn the conduct
of the miners' leaders, telling them that the social system is based on duty,
not on right.[145] Temple's *The Pilgrim* seemed dismayed by the whole affair.
It lectured the government for thinking in terms of industrial warfare but
referred to Baldwin as a "true Christian statesman." The journal pegged its
hopes for continued industrial peace on the Sankey Commission.

The government's resolve was made firmer by the Strike. For labor, it
produced weakness, apathy and an ad unwillingness to take up industrial
action again. And, while trade union membership fell off, workers became
more loyal to the Labour Party.[146] In short, the government was confirmed
in its stay-put stance, the labor movement suffered a severe setback and

Christian interventionists were invited to rethink their strategies of providing social guidance out of the resources of the faith.

Ever attentive to the careful explication of the faith once delivered, the Anglo-Catholic party brought out, in the year of the Strike, an ad ambitious series of seventeen volumes called Anglo-Catholic Books, under the general editorship of Reginald Tribe and Percy Widdrington and with an ad introduction by Charles Gore. The series is notable both for the wide range of its subjects and for the fact that it included a significant number of books on social and economic applications of Christian dogma.

In *The Church and the Kingdom of God* Widdrington lifted up his apologetic interest, remarking that the phrase "Kingdom of God" had become known by the average person and could thus be used as a gateway to the faith . However, it must be correctly defined. Congruently with the American social gospel movement, he argued that it is not "the ethical teaching of the Gospels divorced from any belief in the Personality of our Lord and the Mission of the Church."[147] Nor is it another name for the church, a description of foreign missionary enterprises nor a symbol for the reward of the faithful after death. It entails, rather, the belief in a purpose informing life, stands for a moral ideal and is a canon by which to judge the social value of religious organizations. Widdrington wrote in the Maurician tradition, although he did not mention his mentor, and it is interesting to note that he apparently felt no need, as Maurice had, to demonstrate that the social dimension was part of the Kingdom idea in the New Testament. He simply asserts it.

One of the most competent, well written and scholarly books in the 1926 series was *The Social Teaching of the Post-Reformation Church* by Ruth Kenyon, later prominent in Christendom circles. She demonstrated that the church's concern for the social order is not a novelty but was solidly part of the Middle Ages. Thus for Kenyon a social theology was not a Protestant innovation but an integral part of the catholic tradition.

Other volumes treated the social teaching of the early church, medieval economics and the social teaching of the Oxford Movement (to which everyone seemed to wish to lay claim), the liturgical year (by Prof. Vida Scudder, a leading social gospel advocate in America) and the Mass (by Kenneth Ingram, a barrister, who moved away from Anglo-Catholicism in the late thirties).

The series is emblematic of Anglo-Catholicism in this period, demonstrating its intellectual vigor, the "catholic" range of its interests and its strength within the English Church. It is also emblematic of the period itself. The notes of crisis and chaos, sounded repetitively in the thirties, are not sounded in these volumes. In a time when the nation was setting about resolutely to rebuild and reshape after the war, the church was suggesting how that rebuilding and reshaping might proceed Christianly.

The third Anglo-Catholic Congress took place in 1927, enrolling 21,000 and raising £23,000 for various projects. Its theme was the Eucharist but very little was said about the social implications of the Mass.[148] This was the era of Prayer Book revision; the church was in the process of deciding which revision to recommend to Parliament, which ended up rejecting all of them on two occasions. It was a frustrating time for everyone; the debate sapped energy, evoked bitterness and left scant space on Congress or Convocation programs for discussion of larger things.[149]

William Temple was an energetic actor in the Prayer Book controversy but he still found time in 1927 to assemble material from *The Pilgrim* and to publish it under the title *Essays in Christian Politics and Kindred Subjects*. In it, he ranged over a variety of topics and in his treatment of them a number of his fundamental motifs emerge. As has been mentioned above, one of these is the idea of fellowship. It is "the moral achievement of the Labour Party," he wrote, "that it has made fellowship the ideal of a political party."[150] The mutuality of fellowship is an ad outstanding feature of the Kingdom of God, another extremely important element of Temple's theology. From the vantage of the Kingdom, Temple said, in which all are equal, the class antagonism unfortunately fostered by the Labour Party creates a spurious fellowship.[151] His commendation of the Party reflects one dimension of the Kingdom: it is in some sense and way already manifested in the temporal sphere. His criticism reflects another: as an ad eschatological entity, it is not fully manifest anywhere; its realization calls forth moral effort. For Temple, as for Maurice, the Kingdom is the "great existing reality." To grasp it is to grasp the principles upon which life, politics and society are to be based.[152]

Closely related to the ideas of Kingdom and fellowship in Temple's thought is that of service. Industry is cooperation for public service, he noted in 1927; those who treat it only as a field for private gain are looking at it in a false, unreal way. This subordination of profit to service is one of the incontrovertible principles of socialism, Temple wrote, which all Christians ought to acknowledge.[153] To serve the heavenly King is not to be separated from service to fellow humans here on earth. The Kingdom summons all parties and persons in society to cooperate (a key term) for the common weal, with the Kingdom standing ever as a critique of any concrete, i.e., political steps toward its realization. Adducing the parable of the sower, Temple repeatedly stressed the gradual, progressive character of the Kingdom's coming; thus he was critical of American social gospel activists in their neglect of the Kingdom's eschatological aspect.[154] Yet he was no apocalyptist and he underscored the necessity of human effort in the cause of justice. He argued, again with Maurice, that moral progress is a fact, the root of humanity being in Christ and not, *contra* Barth, in Adam.[155] All people can evince to some degree the Spirit of Christ and can therefore actively make way for the Kingdom; the church is not the Spirit's sole sphere of influence. The church, through its praying, its thinking and, especially, its self-sacrificing example (this is a persistent theme in Temple), can influence matter with spirit (another important theme, from Plato *via* Caird and Green). Temple, however, does not go as far as had some social gospel preachers in America, judging the church's validity instrumentally, only in terms of its eleemosynary or political effectiveness.[156] In the Tractarian tradition, he held to the divine nature of the church and its essential validity apart from pragmatic criteria. Preaching basic principles is its chief contribution to the welfare of the *polis* and it puts forth specific proposals, when it does, modestly and with less confidence than it asserts the faith's fundamentals.[157]

Temple also adverted, in his 1927 book, to the notion of the state as a moral educator which, as noted above, derived from Plato. This is a theme common to Christian social commentators across the spectrum: they were not only interested in a reformed society but in a society which reforms, i.e., encourages the values of fellowship, cooperation and reverence for individual personality, thus making it easier for people to rise to high ethical standards. Indeed, as Temple maintained, with Plato, the person is immortal, the state impermanent. Therefore the state exists to serve the people. "The end of the state is freedom," i.e., each person's liberty to attaint to his or her loftiest ends, divinely decreed.[158] And Temple here very forcefully defends the divine provenance of the state; it is this doctrine alone, he asserts, that can limit the state's power and call it to its true, human purposes.[159]

The year 1927 saw the failure of the Conference on Naval Disarmament, which moved the issue of peace to the fore on the League of the Church Militant's agenda. A. Maude Royden was worried that the League of Nations was accepting the balance-of-power principle which it had come into being to supplant. There was, she felt, too much secret diplomacy occurring, rather than free discussion among those who were publicly accountable. It is up to the citizens to be informed, she exhorted her readers in the "careless twenties" (Graves and Hodge), and to take leaders, like Chamberlain, to task.[160]

Francis Underhill contributed a supportive, upbeat article on the League to *Green Quarterly* but the focus of most Christian social thinkers, in this magazine and elsewhere, was on the domestic scene. Arthur Gardner wrote on penal reform and the literarily prolific Kenneth Ingram argued for the legitimacy of artificial methods of conception control. Likewise, the authors of the Copec pamphlet series, brought out in 1927, underscored domestic social issues, although the foreward mentions that an ad important feature of the times is hope, in varying degrees, for the League. H. G. Wood, in a solid, balanced treatment, set the pace by urging good thinking on the matter of industrial conflict. He cautioned socialists not to think that all great fortunes are made by depriving the ordinary worker of the wealth he or she produces. This represented an overstatement by Marx, who was guilty of black-and-white thinking and the father of "a creed outworn."[161] Rather than competition, union vs. Employer, cooperation (again, the buzzword) is required. Wood wrote with careful, critical instincts similar to those we will note below in Josiah Stamp; and he wrote in the temper of chastened hope that accompanied many on their journey to the thirties: "The cooperative commonwealth is within our reach if we belong to the ranks of the men of goodwill."[162]

The year 1928 saw the voting age for women lowered from thirty to twenty one, the "Flapper Vote." It marked the latest in a series of advances on the feminist front. In 1923, wives were given the right to divorce their husbands on the grounds of adultery alone, with the father having access to the children only if he were a "desirable influence." The Married Women Property Act of 1925 made husbands and wives separate individuals in any financial transaction. Social change could be felt in the factory as well as in the home. While the League of the Kingdom of God *Quarterly* was calling upon the "forces of Christendom to mediate in the warfare between capital and labour," Mondism, in the form of the Mond-Turner talks was effecting some industrial peace. Despite protest from the left, cooperation between employers and employed continued up to the Crash and was revived, in the nineteen eighties, under pressure from foreign competition and following another disastrous miners' strike. Some measure of peace also seemed attainable on the international level; in August, 1928, representatives of fifteen powers met in Paris to sign the popular Kellog-Briand Pact for the Renunciation of War.

Perhaps the most significant contribution to Christian social thought in this relatively tranquil period was by Temple, in his Scott Holland Memorial Lectures, published as *Christianity and the State* in 1928. He traced the history of Christian social concern, which emerged in simple reaction to economic distress but quickly began to investigate systemic problems. For Temple, the path to ethnically sensitive politics had already been pointed out to the church by Plato, who emphasized the educative value of society. The medieval synthesis was not the best expression of the Platonic principle, however, because it was sclerotic, unable to accommodate new knowledge. Hence for Art and Science to be free, the synthesis had to be destroyed and Theology enthroned. Citing Machiavelli as the exemplar of the post-medieval emancipation of politics from religious control, Temple charted the tradition through Hobbes, Locke and Rousseau to the complete secularization of politics and the deification of the state in Hegel. His hero was Spinoza. Having accepted the Machiavellian starting points, he reached the conclusions of St. Augustine and is "the one modern philosopher who is worthy to be named in the same breath as Plato."[163]

Here we see mature religious social thought, exemplified by Temple, which has moved far beyond reaction to Industrial Revolution distress, scattered reformist activism and the mere search for economic amelioration, which colored some quarters of the American social gospel movement. Temple liked Spinoza for a number of reasons. He closely links politics and metaphysics. He grounds the state in what is deepest in human nature, the source, in turn, of all that is the best in it. In contrast to Hobbes' focus on selfishness, Spinoza holds up the ideal, although he faces facts and is no utopian. In Spinoza, Temple suggested, Christian social thinkers have a worthy ally.

Christianity and the State is remarkable for its philosophical breadth but also for its deep criticism of Middle Ages nostalgia, a theme to which its author would return in his Gifford Lectures, *Nature, Man and God* four years later. At a time when Edward Major, in the *Modern Churchman*, was complaining that "whilst the people are becoming Modernist, not a few of the English clergy are becoming Medievalist" at a ratio of five to one,[164] Temple was pointing out that the era's problems were being stated in ways much different than they were in Thomas Aquinas' day. Also, moderns entertain a post-Enlightenment historical perspective, "the real distinction of the modern mind."[165] For Temple, the way forward was not the way back, as it was for some of his friends. These included people associated with the Christendom Group. Their brand of neo-Thomism was very evident at Malvern, in 1941, and Temple lent his support to them as he did to so many others. Yet he was far from a merely indulgent supporter of their romantic medievalism.

Another Temple friend, whom he supported through a highly controversial career, was his Dean at Manchester, Hewlett Johnson. The

latter wrote *Religion Interferes*, "an uncensored talk on Christianity and the
purchaser," in 1928. It was a good example of how the Christian social
movement often failed to rise to the high standards set for it by the Bishop
of Manchester.   Johnson in this piece was closer in style to some
practically-minded American writers than he was to his philosophically
oriented British colleagues.   Religion has to do with relationships, he
asserted and so does commerce: the two can't be separated.   The root
principle in both is service, not gain.   But, according to Johnson's simplistic
analysis, the mutual service ideal is obscured by the "profit motive."[166]
Religion must be rescued from being only a department of life (a familiar
contention), Johnson argued, and cited as a sign of hope the Co-Operative
Movement, "founded by men who believed in Christian values."[167]
Johnson's book shows that at least some religious thinkers were attempting
to speak to an ad audience wider than the church, although much of the
period's writing carries a decidedly "in house" air.   It was one offering in
a "Self and Society" series that, long before the advent of American
consumer advocates, showed concern about the consumer, "who is every
one of us."   Philip Snowden, Mrs. Sydney Webb, Harold Laski, Walter
Citrine, Margaret Bondfield, Leonard Woolf and other leftish notables
contributed to the series, coordinated, apparently, by Sir Ernest Benn.

The Benn firm also brought out, in 1928 and 1930, another series of thirty
three essays that included some authors not associated with Christianity.   It
was titled *Affirmations: God in the Modern World* and was edited by Percy
Dearmer.   The volume indicates that not all Christian reflection was being
done in isolation from secular currents of thought and that the war and its
aftermath had presented British society with a kind of common agenda.
Dominating that agenda were issues of international peace and a just social
order.[168]

The year 1928 was also notable for the publication of Charles Gore's
1927 Halley Stewart Lectures, *Christ and Society*.   In the book he alluded
to the "dissatisfaction and alarm" pervading society but noted, with good
reason, that the church's response was weakened by vagueness in ideas and
uncertainty in methods.[169]   Gore advocated a thorough rethinking of
Christian ethics, centering on personal morality and the life of fellowship.
He offered his applause for the League of Nations, sternly denounced the
conception control movement and cautioned against the inclination toward
re-establishing the medieval synthesis.   Much of the book is given over to
a historical survey and to the enunciation of general principles.   It contains,
however, two appendices, one, "A Scheme of Industrial Reconstruction
Proposed from New Zealand" (decentralization, workers-as-partners), the

other, by the Council of Christian Ministers on Social Questions, urging the government to raise the school leaving age to fifteen. It also supported the Blanesburgh Report which called for job training for unemployed youth.

Christ and Society neatly reflects what Dean Inge called "The Gore-Temple axis." The former refers to the latter's Scott Holland Lectures a number of times and traverses much of his territory. The volume is a symbol of what was happening in the Christian social movement near the end of the twenties: the leadership was passing from those who knew the old days of Maurice and Westcott to those who would take the movement into World War II and the Welfare State and into the World Council of Churches.

"One of the most prominent features of recent religious history," Temple noted in 1928, "has been the steadily increasing effort to recover something like a real Christian sociology."[170] A representative sample of that effort came out the following year in *A Plea for Christian Sociology* by P. T. R. Kirk, then working for the centrist Industrial Christian Fellowship. In this pamphlet, Kirk was not attempting a thoroughgoing repristination of the medieval social order on the basis of Thomistic principles. Rather, he was putting forward an ad irenic cluster of ideas which could be subscribed by a majority of the faithful.

For Kirk, as it was for Maurice, the starting point is the Incarnation. Extrapolated from that doctrine are three "social meanings": 1) The Sacredness of Human Personality, the Fatherhood of God, Brotherhood of Man. All humans, consecrated by Christ, deserve liberty and their lives count for more than property. They cannot be regarded as "hands" and it is industry's first duty to pay workers a living wage. They should have adequate leisure, housing and sanitation and relief from monotonous work; 2) The Spiritual or Sacramental Value of Material Things. If God is anywhere, he must be everywhere. (This sacramental emphasis, which is also Maurician, did not lead Kirk to an ad Anglo-Catholic interpretation, along the lines of Conrad Noel or Studdert Kennedy.[171] Nor did it lead him into a sentimental naturalism: the message of the Father can perhaps be apprehended, Kirk thought, in "the face behind the gentle caress of high-powered industrial machines."[172] Their utility is to be judged by their value to humans, not by the products they produce); 3) Fellowship Motivated by Love. Kirk recognized the difficulty of applying this principle in, e.g., industrial disputes. But he was rather sunnily confident that difficulties could be easily solved on the basis of restored goodwill; 4) All Life is Service. All toil, all industry is to be directed teleologically, toward the community's benefit, not engaged in only for private gain. In this connection he noted the proliferation of industries producing only luxurious or harmful goods, a concern that was beginning to emerge at this time of ramification for British manufacturing.

Not all was serene on the manufacturing scene in 1929, as reflected in V. A. Demant's *The Miners' Distress and the Coal Problem.* This study was brought out by the ecumenical Christian Social Council, which had been formed the year previous by Ruth Kenyon, Reginald Tribe, Malcolm Spencer and other and of which Demant was research director.   And Demant in fact argued that too much Christian social comment is based on inadequate information. To redress that imbalance he alluded to surveys of distressed (soon to be labeled, euphemistically, special) areas of high unemployment, quoting experts such as the aptly-named Dr. H. A. Mess.[173] For the author, the solution to the coal problem lay in the direction of nationalization or rationalization, with the government taking the initiative in either case.

 Demant's book is theologically thin and in it, "Christian conscience" seems to mean "sensitive conscience" only. The church, its conscience troubled, can respond by encouraging direct relief of miners' families, insist on security for those working in the industry and encourage "any" measures to relieve unemployment, even the "temporary and palliative."[174] A major motif in Demant's approach to economic problems in the thirties emerges here: there are no iron economic laws (*contra Cunningham and Headlam*); people and their decisions are determinative. And the book gives off a whiff, however faint, of the tension and sense of crisis that would become eminently stronger in the next decade.

That sense of crisis was precipitated, of course, by the Crash of October, 1929.   The previous June had witnessed the formation of a Labour government with Margaret Bondfield becoming the first woman cabinet minister (labor).   W. G. Peck was impressed by the moral strength of the Labour administration[175] while S. C. Carpenter lamented that may Labour politicians, although practicing Christians, were uninterested in theology.[176] Few in any party, except those friends of cartoonist David Low's Col. Blimp who were shocked at his "socialism," objected to William Temple's enthronement at York.   Yet any rejoicing was subdued in those days, although perhaps not among the many in southern England who were able to keep the distressed areas, mainly in the north, out of their daily purview. But for the socially aware, Christian or not, the lofty post-war hopes for reconstruction at home and for a new, pacific international order, had come to a pretty pass.

They were beginning to understand what "the great disillusionment" was all about.

Notes

1. Bentley B. Gilbert, *British Social Policy 1914-1919* (Ithaca: Cornell University Press, 1970), p. 8.

2. "In an era of change and uncertainty, he was a reminder of steadier and happier times." From a review of Kenneth Rose's *King George V* (London: Weidenfeld and Nicholson, 1983) by Carolly Erickson in the *Los Angeles Times Book Review*, May 27, 1984.

3. Maurice Reckitt, *Faith and Society* (London: Longmans, Green, 1932), p. 108.

4. Gilbert, *op. cit.*, p. 1.

5. Masterman, *op. cit.*, p. 1.

6. *Ibid.*, p. 24.

7. *Ibid.*, p. 11.

8. John Stevenson, *British Society 1914-1945* (London: Pelican Books, 1984), p. 34. The possession of servants was Seebohm Rowntree's 1901 criterion for distinguishing between the working and middle classes.

9. *Ibid.*, p. 106.

10. Masterman, *op. cit.*, p. 76.

11. Stevenson, *op. cit.*, p. 107.

12. Masterman, *op. cit.*, p. 100.

13. *Ibid.*, p. 200.

14. *Ibid.*, p. 201. Masterman believed that his Liberalism was consonant with the goals of the Labour Party, including a living wage, decent housing, limited hours and unemployment insurance. He was, however, an elitist, advocating government by an "aristocracy of intelligence." See his *The New Liberalism* (London: Leonard Parsons, 1920), pp. 137-8 and 213. Dean Inge also noted the interest in "necromancy" that reminded him that "improvement in education has not been accompanied by any intrinsic advance in the intelligence of the people." See *England* (London: Hodder and Stoughton, 1926), p.91 (sixth printing, 1938).

15. *Ibid.*, p. 202.

16. Will Reason, *Christianity and Social Renewal* (London: SCM Press, 1919), p. 12.

17. *Ibid.*, p. 25.

18. *Ibid.*, p. 62.

19. Robert Graves and Alan Hodge, *The Long Weekend* (New York: Macmillan, 1941), p. 7.

20. *Ibid.*, p. 5.

21. G. A. Studdert Kennedy, *Democracy and the Dog Collar* (London: Hodder and Stoughton, 1921), p. 4.

22. *Ibid.*, p. 61.

23. *Ibid.*, p. 99.

24. Woodbine Willie's popularity was exceptional. Graves and Hodge (*op. cit.*, p. 5): most chaplains were regarded as "comic turns" and elsewhere Graves says flatly, "Anglican chaplains were remarkably out of touch with their troops." (*Goodby to All That* [London: Penguin, 1983, first published by Jonathan Cape, 1929]), p. 159.

25. Stevenson, *op. cit.*, p. 364.

26. In May, 1913, the Church League for Women's Suffrage published a statement of principles, with St. Margaret on the cover. It was supported by six bishops; the names of social Christian stalwarts Paul Bull, T. C. Gobat, Henry Scott Holland, G. D. Rosenthal and N. E. Edgerton Swann were also appended. Membership was reported to be 310. I have no evidence that this particular League survived the war; it seems to have merged into the League of the Church Militant, with its *Monthly* becoming *The Church Militant*. The latter League seems itself to have disappeared by 1928.

27. F. A. Iremonger, *William Temple: Archbishop of Canterbury* (London: Oxford University Press, 1948), p. 454.

28. *Ibid.*, p. 450.

29. *Church Quarterly Review*, October, 1920. Conservative editor Headlam, writing in the January number, expressed his disapproval of the "socialism of the war," denouncing the increased taxation and heavy-handed government that came from what Maurice Bruce has called Lloyd-George's "series of magnificent improvisations." (*The Coming of the Welfare State* [London: B. T. Batsford, 1965], p. 17).

30. Charles Gore, *Christianity Applied to the Life of Men and of Nations* (London: John Murray, 1920), p. 10 (1940 edition).

31. *Ibid..*, p. 17.

32. *Ibid.*, p. 18.

33. *Ibid..*, p. 24.

34. *Ibid.*, p. 28.

35. Quoted in Iremonger, *op. cit.*, p. 322.

36. Quick was influenced in his theological development by Inge, Von Hü gel and Evelyn Underhill but, unlike Inge, he eschewed the role of curmudgeonly controversialist. His several apologetical works, using Plato as a point of departure and advocating a kenotic Christology reflecting Gore's, were widely read. At the height of his powers in the late twenties (he published the weighty *The Christian Sacraments* in 1927), he was regarded as somewhat eccentric in his later years and died in 1944. See "Oliver Quick as a Theologian," a reprint from *Theology* by J. K. Mozley, published by SPCK in 1945.

37. The phrase is from S. T. Glass, *The Responsible Society* (London: Longmans, Green, 1966).

38. *The Pilgrim*, 7:2, January, 1927.

39. Hannington's often colorful story is in his book *Unemployed Struggles 1919-1936* (York: E. P. Publishing, 1936).

40. *The Chronicle of Convocation* (London: SPCK, 1921), p. 597.

41. Kenneth Ingram, *Basil Jellicoe* (London: The Centenary Press, 1936), Foreward.

42. *Ibid.*, p. 58. The prayer group Jellicoe formed to intercede for the Society was called Servants of the Manger.

43. R. H. Tawney, *The Acquisitive Society* (London: G. Bell, 1921), p. 2.

44. For an excellent discussion of the philosophical background to classical Liberalism, see Harold J. Laski, *The Decline of Liberalism* (London: Oxford University Press, 1940).

45. Tawney, *op. cit.*, pp. 21-22.

46. *Ibid.*, p. 101.

47. *Ibid.*, p. 224.

48. *Ibid.*, p. 228.

49. Tawney seemed to have derived the notion of "industry as service" from Ruskin and put it forward, without attribution, already in a 1918 essay, "The Conditions of Economic Reality." See R. H. Tawney, *The Radical Tradition* (London: John Murray, 1964).

50. Stanley Pierson, *British Socialists* (Cambridge: Harvard University Press, 1979), p. 346.

51. G. Clive Binyon, *The Christian Faith and the Social Revolution* (London: SPCK, 1921), p. 3.

52. No one seems to be able to pinpoint when or where Sir William uttered these oft-quoted words but they are quoted, significantly, *in Fabian Essays* for 1920. See A. R. Vidler, *F. D. Maurice and Company* (London: SCM Press, 1966), p. 259.

53. Binyon, *op. cit.*, p. 12.

54. *Ibid.*, p. 44.

55. *Ibid.*, p. 39.

56. *The Pilgrim, op. cit.*, 1:2, p. 126.

57. Some years before, after the Easter Rebellion of 1916, Conrad Noel had placed the Sinn Fein flag alongside the Red Flag and the Flag of St. George in Thaxted Church. He chronicled the ensuing brouhaha in *The Battle of the Flags* (1922).

58. *The Pilgrim, op. cit.*, 1:3, p. 241.

59. *Ibid.*, p. 311. Deane alluded to the intense hostility directed by some against the medievalism of the Anglo-Catholics. This theme, an important one, is explored in the next chapter, with particular reference to the Christendom Group.

60. C. L. Mowat, *Britain Between the Wars* (London: Methuen, 1955), p. 222.

61. In his book *Our Social Heritage* (New Haven: Yale University Press, 1921), Graham Wallas opined that Anglo-Catholicism was already the most powerful force in the Anglican Church (p. 259). Son of an Anglican clergyman, Wallas was a powerful intellectual presence among his contemporaries; this volume, however, is curiously scattered and unconvincing and seems to have been written to the sound

of grinding axes.

62. See McEwan Lawson, *God's Back-Room Boy* (London: Lutterworth Press, 1952). Free Church missionary to India C. F. Andrews was another prominent writer on social and economic topics. In *Christ and Labour* (London: SCM Press, 1923), he looks with simplistic nostalgia at the Middle Ages while touching on standard social Christian themes. Paul Bull's critique, from a self-conscious Anglo-Catholic perspective, scored Andrews' weak Christology (*Chronicle* of the Community of the Resurrection).

63. Ms. Gardner served as matchmaker for Temple: he met his future bride, Frances Anson, at a Christmas party she hosted in the "Collegium" house on St. George's Square. See Iremonger, *op. cit.*, p. 197.

64. *Ibid.*, p. 334.

65. Maldwyn Edwards, *S. E. Keeble* (London: Epworth Press, 1949), p. 46.

66. *Ibid.*, p. 90.

67. King says that no one of Hughes' stature succeeded him and, thus, social Christianity languished in Nonconformity. In view of S. E. Keeble's stature, this is perhaps an overstatement.

68. Edwards, *op. cit.*, p. 44.

69. S. E. Keeble, *Christian Responsibility for the Social Order* (London: Epworth press, 1922), p. 120.

70. *Ibid.*, p. 134.

71. An alternative view, citing Christian involvement, is presented in James Haslam, ed., *The People's Yearbook* (Manchester and Glasgow: The Cooperative Wholesale Society, 1928), p. 14.

72. Keeble, *op. cit.*, p. 155.

73. This was one result of the famous Geddes Axe, which had been laid to the root of the tree of government overspending in 1921. (A waggish journalist suggested that "Geddes" was the plural of "God"). *The Pilgrim* welcomed the Geddes Report, agreeing with its conclusion that the budget was bloated. In line with Temple's steady concern for education, however, it cautioned restraint in this area (2:3).

74. Other lectureships that invited speakers to address social issues from Christian points of view were the Fernley (later, Fernley-Hartley), Beckley and Halley-Stewart. Holders of the Scott Holland Lectureship on "the Religion of the Incarnation in its bearing on the social and economic life of man" in the period were Tawney, C. E. Osborne, Temple, A. D. Lindsay, W. H. Moberly and S. C. Carpenter.

75. R. H. Tawney, *Religion and the Rise of Capitalism* (London: John Murray, 1926), p. 285.

76. *Ibid.*., pp. 282-3.

77. In a thoughtful article in *Modern Churchman*, 26:1, 1983, titled "Is There a Theology of Equality?" Ronald Bowlby rightly points to the "illusive, yet necessary" character of the idea of equality; he also notes, correctly, that it does not assume prominence in the thought of Temple, who was more inclined to emphasize fellowship.

78. Tawney, *op. cit.*, p. 19.

79. W. H. Greenleaf, *The British Political Tradition, Vol. 2* (London and New York: Methuen, 1983), p. 413. Greenleaf's hand is steady when he writes on political topics but less so when he discusses religion.

80. Tawney, *op. cit.*, p. 18. Tawney's analysis of the Middle Ages was weakened by his inadequate treatment of Luther. To make him into a great exemplar of individualistic Protestantism, e.g., is to indulge in caricature. Tawney's work is but one instance of the general difficulty British thinkers have in appreciating the complexity of the Saxon reformer.

81. Maurice Reckitt, *P. E. T. Widdrington* (London: SCM Press, 1961), p. 77.

82. Maurice Reckitt, *As It Happened* (London: J. M. Dent, 1941), p. 261.

83. The main thrust of the argument of *Return* can be found in condensed form in a 1922 SCM pamphlet by Reckitt titled *Your Part in the Kingdom.* One reviewer saw it as a sign of the times, a return to idealism after the disillusionment of the war. He wondered, however, if some articles, dealing with traditional doctrinal matters, were offered as sops to conservatives who might otherwise reject out of hand its more radical proposals. Citing Reckitt's two essays, he wondered if the new movement would "burden itself with a mass of disputable history and antiquated philosophy." *Modern Churchman*, December, 1922, p. 523.

84. *See Chronicle of Convocation* for the years 1922-3.

85. Walter Rauschenbusch felt it necessary to write a theology *for* the social gospel movement which, presumably, was already in operation (cf. the title of his 1917 volume).

86. E. H. Carr, *What is History?* (London: Penguin, 1982; first published by Macmillan, 1961), p. 88.

87. *Report of the First Anglo-Catholic Congress* (London: SPCK, 1920), p. 58.

88. *Ibid.*, p. 60.

89. *Ibid.*, p. 61.

90. *Ibid.*, p. 62.

91. *Ibid.*, p. 195.

92. *Ibid.*, p. 196.

93. Francis Underhill and Charles Scott Gillett, ed., *Report of the 1923 Anglo-Catholic Congress* (London: Society of SS. Peter and Paul, 1923), p. 185. The Congresses were not held annually and the gathering of 1923 was the second.

94. *Ibid.*, p. 99. Slesser also contributed a very vague, generalized article on "Christ and Society" to the September, 1922 number of *Theology* in which he contrasted the present social order unfavorably with that of the Middle Ages.

95. *Ibid.*, p. 149. By the early 1980's, passion for social righteousness had largely disappeared from the Anglo-Catholic scene, dislodged by a politically conservative "religion of taste" emphasizing formalism, the Englishness of catholicism and antiquarian tendencies in liturgy, the "idolatry of the fourth century." See Kenneth Leech, *The Social God* (London: Sheldon Press, 1981), p. 22.

96. A sensationalistic example of conservative polemic against social Christianity of the period is H. Musgrave Reade's *Christ or Socialism?* (London: Pickering and Inglis, 1923). His list of "modern cults" against which an "aggressive Christianity" should contend: Socialism, Christian Science, "New Theology," Spiritism, Mormonism, Modernism and Darwinism. Soberer estimations were made by,, e.g., A. C. Headlam in *Church Quarterly Review*.

97. Hewlett Johnson, *Searching for Light* (London: Victor Gollancz, 1968), p. 56.

98. Preston, *op. cit.*, p. 39. Douglas published his ideas in *Credit-Power and Democracy* (London: Cecil Palmer, 1920).

99. *The Pilgrim*, 2:2, January, 1922.

100. A critical review of Johnson's article appeared in the July, 1922 number of *The Pilgrim* over the initials H. A. S. (Slesser). In April, 1923, N. E. Edgerton Swann was saying that, while the Douglas proposal could be challenged, "it can make far stronger claims than any rival program to be *the* Christian solution of the harassing social problem," 3:4(emphasis his).

101. *Ibid.*, 3:3, April, 1923. Number Four, a staple in the teaching of Gandhi and of Martin Luther King, Jr., is not a prominent feature of British Christian social thought between the wars.

102. Gilbert Clive Binyon, *The Social Ideal of the Bible* (Letchworth: G. W. Wardman, 1924), p. vii.

103. *Ibid.*, pp. xiv.-v. Binyon saw the year 1924 as the beginning of a new phase in the Christian social movement, *viz.*, the search for a Christian sociology that derived its axioms and principles from its own dogmatic tradition. He cites Edgerton Swann's 1922 pamphlet "Is There a Christian Sociology?" as inaugurating the phase. See *The Christian Socialist Movement in England* (London: SPCK, 1931), p. 201.

104. Over 500 Church of England priests signed a letter of support sent to MacDonald on March 13, 1923, welcoming the Labour Party as the official opposition. The letter eventually gained 700 signatures; ten signers became bishops. Tawney was happy that a Christian socialist was PM and Temple was glad that the Labour Party would be able to gain experience in governing. That initial learning period was to be extremely short. See *The Pilgrim*, 4:3, April, 1924.

105. Quoted in Iremonger, *op. cit.*, p. 335. Alfred E. Garvie was co-chair but Temple dominated.

106. Roger Lloyd, *The Church of England in the Twentieth Century, Vol. 2* (London: Longmans, Green, 1949), p. 101.

107. *Ibid..*, p. 102.

108. John Oliver, *The Church and Social Order* (London: A. R. Mowbray, 1968), p. 71. An uncontroversial paper, "Historical Illustrations of the Social Effects of Christianity" was also published. The most serious controversy at Copec arose over issues of sexual morality and war. See A. E. Garvie, *Memories and Meanings of My Life* (London: George Allen and Unwin, 1928), p. 75.

109. Oliver, *op. cit.*, p. 74.

110. Edward Shillito, *Christian Citizenship* (London: Longmans, Green, 1924), pp. 5-6.

111. S. E. Keeble, *Copec*, a pamphlet published by Epworth Press, 1924.

112. Maurice Reckitt, *Faith and Society, op. cit.*, p. 127.

113. Philip Mairet, *The National Church and the Social Order* (London: Church Information Board, 1956), p. 117.

114. Herbert Hensley Henson, *Retrospect of an Unimportant Life, Vol. 3* (London: Oxford University Press, 1942), p. 223. Henson, whose predecessor as Dean at Durham was Westcott, was a conservative in the Burkean mold. A vain, sometimes appealing, always highly opinionated controversialist, he harbored ambitions for York.

115. *Modern Churchman*, May, 1924 and January, 1925. Incredibly, Pryke failed to mention Temple in either of his two articles. William Inge was President of the Modern Churchmen's Union at this time.

116. Justus F. Laun, *Social Christianity in England* (London: SCM Press, 1929), pp. 90-92. In his foreward, Temple stressed the influence of English Humanism, the major source of which is Plato, in forging the bonds between religion and society. This led, he wrote, to the "discovery in an ultimate other-worldliness of a spur to reforming action in the present." Copec was, therefore, "more Platonist than anything else," even as it was the classically-trained Temple more than any *one* else in its conclusions.

117. *Theology*, July, 1924. The journal's commentary on social and economic matters was not always of high quality, as witness its oddly scattered review of H. A. Mess' *Studies in the Christian Gospel for Society* in the April, 1924, number. It reflected a conservative point of view. Mess was a Free Churchman and a pacifist.

118. *Chronicle of Convocation*, May, 1924, p. 228.

119. *The Pilgrim*, 4:4, July, 1924. Many Copec speakers were also *Pilgrim* writers. The influential Rudolph Eucken, in this same period, was able to make careful use of medieval insights without a wholesale endorsement of the "historical and romantic movement" back to the past taking place at the time. The religious tone of his work echoes Bernard Bosanquet's. See *The Individual and Society* (London: Faith Press, 1923), p. 43.

120. It is interesting to note that the *Green Quarterly* announced, in its first number, that it would carry articles on social subjects largely in response to Frank Weston's "tabernacle" speech. Social Christianity was not, however, prominent in its pages.

121. A. J. Penty, *Toward a Christian Sociology* (London: George Allen and Unwin, 1923), p. 39. Anti-democratic sentiments are expressed, but not elaborated on, in the book. Penty ended his days with Oswald Mosley's Fascists. C. E. M. Joad identified Penty with the utopian phase of Guild Socialism in the Morris tradition, an idea, Joad wrote, affecting many of the younger Labour leaders. See *Introduction to Modern Political Theory* (Oxford: Clarendon Press, 1924), p. 74.

122. In the relative affluence of the mid-twenties, Royden could score manufacturers of new houses for failing to provide heat for the top floor, where servants lived.

123. The League of the Church Militant, publisher of Royden's pamphlets, may have been a fringe group with unpopular opinions but it worked out of an office in Dean's Yard, Church House, Westminster.

124. Mairet, *op. cit.*, p. 115.

125. Molly Gobat, *T. C. Gobat* (Letchworth: G. W. Wardman, 1938), p. 61. Gobat disputes G. C. Binyon's date of 1924 for the founding of the LKG; Oliver also gives 1924, whereas Stanley Evans sides with Ms. Gobat.

126. LKG meetings must have been fun. Molly Gobat allows that her father would grow weary of the "endless discussion, and snortings from Widdrington and Reckitt." *Ibid.*

127. For a brief sketch of these movements, see Stanley Evans' *Christian Socialism*, a pamphlet published in 1962 by the Christian Socialist Movement. The SSC was organized at a favorite radical hangout, the Food Reform Restaurant, on Furnivall Street, off Holborn. On a visit to London, I tried to locate the eatery and found, alas, only an American-style fast food place.

128. Reckitt, *Faith and Society, op. cit.*, p. 258. In a bland, general, not too profound work, *Christianity and Politics* (London: John Murray, 1925), p. 146, H. W. Fox argued that no party could assert that its principles are the only Christian ones. A. D. Lindsay, too, cited the diversity of Christian opinion as foreclosing the possibility of a religious party. See *The State, the Church and the Community* (London: Copec Central Committee, 1927).

129. The Church Missionary Society, in this period, was urging groups to discuss the issue and to read Oldham's book, but concern was not widespread.

130. J. H. Oldham, *Christianity and the Race Question* (London: SCM Press, 1933), p. 22.

131. *Ibid.*, p. 180.

132. Basil Mathews, *The Clash of Colour* (London: Edinburgh House Press, 1925). Mathews was not favorably disposed toward Gandhi, regarding him as encouraging race separation. An addition to the meager literature from the secular side was a Labour pamphlet, *The Black Man's Rights* by C. R. Buxton, also published in 1925.

133. Alec Vidler has pointed out that Maurice never spoke of pluralism but always of a *Christian* society, a permanent divine order underlying all institutions. See *F. D. Maurice and Company, op. cit.*, p. 178. D. L. Munby has labeled its reluctance openly to face up to its actual divisions a weakness in British society. See *The Idea of a Secular Society* (London: Oxford University Press, 1966), p. 18.

134. Binyon, *The Social Ideal of the Bible, op. cit.*, p. 193.

135. The LKG saw itself as being in succession to Headlam, "the real hero of the movement," as well as to Pusey, Maurice, Kingsley, Westcott, Scott Holland, Hancock and Marson. See the LKG *Quarterly*, 1:1, January, 1926.

136. A. J. P. Taylor, *English History 1914-45* (London: Oxford University Press, 1965), p. 236.

137. *Ibid.*, p. 299. The alliterative label is E. H. Carr's. Reginald F. Rynd, in an article, "The Social Gospel" in *Hibbert Journal*, 24:2, exaggerated the "accession of Anglican clergy to the ranks of Socialism" and condemned its influence among them. This is a superficial, ill-tempered piece, not up to *Hibbert Journal* standards.

138. Stephen Constantine, *Unemployment in Britain Between the Wars* (London: Longmans, 1980), p. 47.

139. *The Pilgrim*, 6:1, October, 1925.

140. *The Pilgrim*, 6:2, January, 1926.

141. R. H. Tawney, *The British Labor Movement* (New Haven: Yale University Press, 1925), p. 148.

142. See a review by Richard Price in *Labor History*, 25:1, Winter, 1984 of Keith Middlemass, *Politics in Industrial Society: The Experience of the British System Since 1911* (Totowa, NJ: Rowan and Littlefield, 1980).

143. Iremonger, *op. cit.*, pp. 337-44.

144. *Green Quarterly*, Summer, 1926. E. R. Norman, *Church and Society in England 1770-1970* (Oxford: Clarendon Press, 1976), p. 338, argues that the public rejected both the form and content of the archiepiscopal intervention.

145. *Church Quarterly Review*, October, 1926.

146. C. L. Mowat, *Britain Between the Wars, op. cit.*, pp. 330-1. The next year, in the Trade Disputes and Trade Unions Act, general strikes were made illegal. Many Christian thinkers were against the bill.

147. Here Widdrington put his finger on an ad issue that touches on the problem of pluralism and was never adequately thought through in the interwar years: to what extent, if at all, can the ethical content of Christian teaching be separated or at least distinguished from its kerygmatic proclamation? It is the question of constructing a public theology in a country with a national church. See, e.g., T. M. Heron's Anglo-Catholic Congress Books offering, *Christian Vocation in Industry and Marketing* in which he writes of "Christian Industry." The question of a specifically Christian contribution to the political tradition is raised in *Seeds of Liberation*, Alistair Kee, ed. (London: SCM Press, 1973), p. 112. A previous series of Congress Books was published in 1923. Out of fifty two pamphlets, only one touched on social topics.

148. An ad appendix on this subject, by Summer School of Sociology coordinator G. D. Rosenthal, was added to the Congress report.

149. Virtually the only outward-looking move by the Anglican Church in assembly occurred in July, 1927, when the Lower House of Canterbury passed a resolution seconding the international sentiment for disarmament and urging membership in the League of Nations Union.

150. William Temple, *Essays in Christian Politics and Kindred Subjects* (London: Longmans, Green, 1927), p. 5.

151. Temple's emphasis on the Kingdom of God can be seen as early as his Repton School days, when he published *The Kingdom of God* (London: Macmillan, 1912). "Christianity begins with the proclamation of the Kingdom of God," he wrote then (p. 40). Temple returned to the theme five years later in a pamphlet *The Coming of the Kingdom* (London: Longmans, Green, 1917); it is a conventional, yet never trite, exegetical study. Still, he applied the Kingdom to labor disputes: imagine if each party came to the table "desiring justice more than advantage."

152. W. R. Rinne, *The Kingdom of God in the Thought of William Temple* (Åbo, Finland: Acta Academiae Åboensis, Ser. A, Vol. 32, No. 1, 1966), p. 72. Rinne's treatment is prolix but shows wide acquaintance with the primary and secondary sources. Joseph Fletcher says that the Kingdom symbol was "a thread that ran consistently through his interpretation of both religious and social questions." See *William Temple: Twentieth Century Christian* (New York: Seabury Press, 1963), p. 35.

153. Temple, *op. cit.*, p. 40.

154. Rinne, *op. cit.*, pp. 75-78.

155. Robert Craig, *Social Concern in the Thought of William Temple* (London: Victor Gollancz, 1963), p.77.

156. Temple also differed in style from some American social gospel preachers, like George M. Heron, whose rhetoric ran to the shrill. Fletcher points out that whereas Walter Rauschenbusch sometimes wrote to rankle, Temple always, true to his dialectical instincts, tried to reconcile apparent opposites (*op. cit.*, p. 229).

157. Rinne, *op. cit.*, p. 86.

158. Temple, *op. cit.*, pp. 39-40.

159. Craig (pp. 102-3) has an ad excellent discussion of Temple's thinking on the state in relation to Emil Brunner's. In contrast to the latter's view, which is very pessimistic, Temple insists that the state is a divine instrument for good, not simply an ad indication of original sin. It is capable of achieving justice, although it is incapable of love. Brunner draws a sharp distinction between the two. Temple, especially in the late thirties, emphasized the Niebuhrian dialectic: love is the fulfillment *and* negation of the artifacts of justice.

160. A. Maude Royden, "Peace-Our Responsibility" (Occasional Papers, *The Church Militant*, 1927).

161. Marxism, as an ad ideology, was never an ad option for anybody but those on the fringe's fringe. But, unlike their American counterparts, British social gospelers took Marx's analysis seriously and were in dialogue with it.

162. Studdert Kennedy's remarkably lucid, forceful, feisty, polemical style is well displayed in his series contribution, *Religion a Blessing or a Curse?* (London: George Allen and Unwin, 1927), p. 106.

163. William Temple, *Christianity and the State* (London: Macmillan, 1928), p. 8.

164. *Modern Churchman*, April, 1928.

165. Temple, *op. cit.*, p. 17.

166. Hewlett Johnson, *Religion Interferes* (London: Ernest Benn, 1928), p. 16.

167. *Ibid.*, p. 38.

168. H. G. Wells wrote of his opposition to the Kellog-Briand Pact, citing its ignoring the sovereign independence of states.

169. Charles Gore, *Christ and Society* (London: George Allen and Unwin, 1928), p. 18.

170. Temple, *op. cit.*, p. 1. Interest in sociology was becoming widespread in this period, as noted by F. J. C. Hearnshaw, *The Development of Political Ideas* (London: Thomas Nelson and Sons, 1937, first published in 1927), p. 144. The book is, among other things, a diatribe against collectivism. Hearnshaw was no fan of Christian socialism, which he breezily dismissed for its "monocular sentimentality" in *A Survey of Socialism* (London: Macmillan, 1928), p. 331.

171. This can be seen in the League of the Kingdom of God's first leaflet, probably published in 1923. It lifts up many of the points raised by Kirk and demonstrates that a notable level of convergence on basic principles could be achieved across party lines at this time in the church.

172. P. T. R. Kirk, *A Plea for a Christian Sociology* (London: Industrial Christian Fellowship, 1929). An ad opposite example is Edward Carpenter, who died in 1929. A former curate of Maurice's, he resigned his orders and lived a back-to-the-land, Thoreauian life. He was, shall we say, a proto-hippie and was deeply suspicious of technology in general and of machines in particular and his "near Luddite attitude" was heavily influential with his contemporaries. See Edward Carpenter, *Edward Carpenter* (London: Dr. Williams's Trust, 1970). Among those he influenced were the busy Katherine and J. Bruce Glasier, propagandists for an ad emotional, ethical socialism and the eponymous subjects of *The Enthusiasts* (London: Victor Gollancz, 1971) by Lawrence Thompson.

173. V. A. Demant, *The Miners' Distress and the Coal Problem* (London: SCM Press, 1929), p. 11. Coal was the largest single employer of labor in the interwar years (Taylor, *op. cit.*, p. 248).

174. Demant, *op. cit.*, p. 70.

175. LKG *Quarterly*, July, 1929. The previous issue had mentioned a visit to the United States by Maurice Reckitt, at the invitation of the Church League for Industrial Democracy (Episcopal), akin, said the journal, to the LKG.

176. S. C. Carpenter, *Democracy in Search of a Religion* (London: SCM Press, 1929), p. 20, fn. An ad exception, perhaps, was Katherine Bruce Glasier, whose 1929 ILP pamphlet "Socialism for Beginners" explicated the Our Father in social terms and argued that only international socialism was in line with the Sermon on the Mount.

Chapter 3

The Thirties

"The stage was set for the drift into the thirties" by the election of 1929, which featured three parties at full strength and resulted in an indecisive Labour victory.[1] The Labour Party's program had been outlined before the Crash in *Labour and the Nation*, R. H. Tawney's popular version of his *The Acquisitive Society.* "Impeccably moral in tone," it was "much vaguer than [Sidney] Webb's program of 1918" and unable to chart a bright course through the gathering gloom.[2] Nor could the Liberal manifesto, *Britain's Industrial Future* of 1929. C. L. Mowat calls the period 1929-31 the "turning point," from the relative calm and prosperity of the twenties to the uncertainty, fear and deprivation of the thirties. Labour's half-measures failed to promote economic recovery and unemployment and social discontent were hallmarks of the decade.[3] Economic recovery could be noticed already by 1935 but the elements of impending doom, highlighted for many in Andre Siegfried's *England's Crisis* of 1930, was never extirpated.

The seventh Lambeth Conference was held in July, 1930. William Temple chaired the Committee on Unity and much time was spent in discussing items of ecumenical import. At a time when the unemployment figure stood at 2.5 million, the bishops managed to reaffirm the Fifth Report and in particular its assertion that cooperation for service, not competition for gain, should be industry's guiding principle. The question of conception control was again taken up; the responsibility of the individual couple for family planning was stressed, although the wide advertisement of contraceptives was frowned upon. Interest was shown in matters economic, with emphasis placed on the function of money and finance, this on the eve of the great financial crisis of 1931 and in line with a steadily growing awareness of financial issues in the general populace at the time. The official Report of the Conference had a complimentary word for Douglas' Social Credit idea but Paul Stacy, writing in *Theology*, found it thin, overall, in economic facts. Criticism came also from W. H. Carnegie who, while lauding the bishops' support for the League of Nations, felt that they did not offer enough specific, practical guidance for the questioning Christian. T. S. Eliot's appraisal reflected a style of thinking that was to pervade intellectual activity in the thirties: the analysis of situations using starkly oppositional categories. For the first time in history since the days of pagan Rome, opined Eliot, attempts were being made to form a civilization entirely apart from the "Christian mentality." This effort, however, he thought destined for failure, with only the church being able to save the world from suicide.[4] For him, the children of light should have no truck with the children of darkness and the distinction between the two was easily discerned.

Eliot expressed satisfaction that Lambeth 1930 reaffirmed the catholicity of the Church of England and ecclesiological topics were much discussed also at the fourth Anglo-Catholic Congress held the same year. Social issues were pushed to the periphery, as could be expected in a setting in which many of the presenters displayed their dependence on the work of Baron F. Von Hügel.[5] It was left for the Congress of 1933, the last before 1940, again the raise the banner of social Christianity. The impact there of Christendom Group thinking was evident in the call for a Christian social philosophy which, for Gabriel Gillett, had always been implicit in the catholic tradition. Several speakers alluded to the slum problem, which was the subject of the Greenwood Act of 1930 and a significant feature of the discussion in Canterbury Convocation. Congress participants were urged by G. D. Rosenthal and by J. G. Lockhart to allow their social consciences to be aroused, reminding them of the precedent set by Dolling, Westcott, Scott Holland, Gore and, of course, by Frank Weston, to whom, it seemed, every speaker was obliged to advert. Little was offered by way of concrete advice, however, with Walter Moncton lamely suggesting that Anglo-Catholics might help the unemployed learn a craft or take up a hobby, to occupy idle time with something worthwhile.

No one was very happy with the shape of things in 1930. The judicious and thoughtful Hugh l'Anson Fausset regarded individualism as the day's central problem, reflected in and fostered by "the ruthless warfare of industrialism."[6] The ever-busy C. E. M. Joad noted a spiritual malaise afflicting the nation, to be seen in the widespread absence of a sense of moral obligation, a retreat from community. With Fausset, he observed the decline in the churches' influence; indeed, the spirit of the age, he thought, invited revolt against all manners and morals of past generations.[7] He was sympathetic to the work of Christian social thinkers in their search for wider angles of vision and in their call for moral passion but he recognized the uphill battle they faced even among their co-religionists.

The Industrial Christian Fellowship's P. T. R. Kirk uttered a similar sentiment. In the church, he wrote about this same time, "we seem to be standing for a kindly and good-natured tolerance of things as they are."[8] One who responded to Kirk's implied challenge and who exerted sustained and strong influence on Christian social thought over the next two decades and beyond was Canon V. A. Demant, research director of the Christian Social Council.[9] In 1931 he widened his earlier concern for miners' welfare into one for the unemployed in general. In his book of that year, *This Unemployment: Disaster or Opportunity?* can be seen both the analytical skills of its author and an indication of the trend of mainstream Christian reaction to economic upheaval.

We are dealing, Demant suggested, not with industrial failure alone but with "one of the major crises in the history of man."[10] Echoing Fausset, he attributed the onset of the crisis to "industrialism," an observation which, for the author, as for many others, did not lead to anything approaching a Marxist position: Demant, e.g., rarely uses the word "capitalism." He was rather interested in uncovering the "inner contradictions" of industrialism, chief among them being that it defeats its own community-service goals. It is unable adequately to distribute the goods it produces nor to keep the producers continuously employed. It exhibits a tension between its technical achievements and "the obsession of scarcity embodied in economic and financial theory.[11] The commanding fallacy is to assume that (*contra* conservatives) adamantine laws govern economic behavior. Industrialism and its unemployment are tractable but to effect change requires political will. Therefore, since Christians ought to be as concerned with truth as with goodness, they should arm themselves facts and nerve themselves for political struggle which, Demant felt, was being viewed as futile by growing numbers of people. Interestingly, political activity was not prominently associated with the Christendom Group, in which Demant was extremely active.

Demant's book demonstrated how hard the social Christian movement had to fight for its legitimacy within the church. Few would argue that there was no crisis, nor that there were no Christian principles which might guide the conduct of people in business and industry. Yet what was not by any means universally accepted was the proposition that theological thinking must move, in Reckitt's phrase, "from ethics to sociology" and *This Unemployment* is peppered with appeals for the inclusion of social and economic analysis in religious reflection. In fact, a good deal of the book is given over to straight economics and presentations of the work of experts like Hawtrey, Hobson and Beveridge.

A major defect of Demant's book was its lengthy defense of the Douglas scheme to bring credit under community control, "as a reflection of its economic possibilities."[12] While many Christian thinkers were not attracted to the Social Credit nostrum, the fear that religious thought would result in a mere wan seconding of secular ideas kept many from taking the more mainstream authorities they quoted completely seriously either. Their attempts at faithful prophetic commentary on the issues of the day were not untinged by a utopian romanticism that traditionally tinges much secular British socialist thought.[13] [14]

The year 1931 was a momentous one for Great Britain. The country, according to Samuel Beer, was entering a crucial period, which would last until 1935 and issue in the founding of the managed economy.[15] The country went off the gold standard in September and the trend toward increasing cutbacks was clearly seen.[16] One result was the introduction of the despised Means Test, which spread much material and mental hardship in working class areas throughout what came to be called the Slump. Another was the August break-up of the Labour government over the question of reducing unemployment benefits. This gave rise to the coalition National government, the formation of which was etched forever in Labourite minds as Ramsay MacDonald's "sell-out." The new government faced the same problems as had the old and had little to offer by way of remedy. The previous year one charismatic Labour figure, Oswald Mosley, had proposed his own remedies for the unemployment disease, but they were rejected. He proceeded to quit the government and founded the New Party, which transmogrified itself in 1932 into the blackshirted British Union of Fascists. And on the international scene the most ominous news, aside from the financial crisis and the Slump itself, was the Japanese invasion of Manchuria...ominous not only for the hapless Manchurians but for the world. The League of Nations did nothing but bluster and talk and with its manifest impotence in the face of aggression, the nations moved closer to war.

Of the largest significance for Christian social thought in Great Britain was the founding, in the watershed year 1931, of *Christendom*. The journal was begun by people associated with the League of the Kingdom of God: Reckitt, Percy Widdrington, Demant, Kenyon, L. S. Thornton, W. G.

Peck and Henry Slesser were prominent. It was supported financially by Reckitt and by the Buxton Trust, with some money coming from the LKG. Through the efforts of Widdrington, the journal sponsored the first Christendom Conference in 1932 at a house, "Moreton," in St. Leonard's-on-Sea owned by Gore's Community of the Resurrection at Mirfield. Out of these conferences grew the Christendom Group, which was to have a large impact at the Malvern Conference in 1941. The Group continued to meet into the war years; the journal perdured until 1950.[17]

In the background of the Christendom movement[18] lies the Church Socialist League, out of which had come the LKG, founded by those in the CSL who were moving away from the idea of public ownership of the means of production and toward a more catholic cast to the faith. The collectivist minority in the CSL established the Society of Socialist Christians, as has been mentioned. It later became the Socialist Christian Fellowship, with George Lansbury as president.[19]

It is perhaps too much to say that the Christendom Group stood for out-and-out medieval escapism; its members were constantly at pains to refute precisely that charge. But they were deeply disturbed by the social chaos they saw on every side, by a trend toward secular statism and by the instability of the international order. Their greatest perceived enemy was ambiguity and unclarity of thought and they rose eagerly to Demant's summons to move from heart to brain; from purely negative revulsion at industrialism to a positive social philosophy for the reinvention of civilization. Under the spell of a Thomistic revival which had been generated in part by the publication of the encyclical *Aeterni Patris* in 1897, they returned repeatedly for inspiration to medieval images of a common culture, a shared faith. Their search for relief from ambiguity, for solid grounding when all seemed up for grabs, their aversion to history and to modernity, led them to the authoritative Aristotelian theology of Western catholicism and to the authoritative social order that exemplified it. In the language of Paul Tillich, who was writing on these matters at this time, they broke the dialectical tension between "whither" and "whence" by opting for the former, the "myth of origin."[20] They became political romantics.

With their wayward brilliance, rudderless philosophical facility and felicitous style of expression, the Christendom people influenced those, like Temple, who could speak their categorical and conceptual language, but their Christian intellectualist elitism made them insular and kept them isolated from broader, more mainstream currents of thought. They wished passionately to discover a social philosophy that would stand on its own Christian legs; that passion caused them, often, to stand alone, apart from those whose journey to a more humane *polis* took them in directions other than the medievalist *civitatis Dei* shy both of modernity and machinery. Ronald Preston's judgment rights true: they overestimated the degree to which society was Christian.[21] Still, in the drifting thirties, groping as they did for a steady course, they were very much like their fellow travelers outside the church in two important respects: they lived fully in an atmosphere of crisis that pervaded the decade and they looked for resolution in intellectual postures that tended toward the totalist and uncompromising.

I devote significant attention to the journal *Christendom* because it was a major feature of the social Christian landscape in the period (and still, in another form, wields influence) and because it is little know on this side of the Atlantic.

The tone was set in the statement of purpose carried in the journal's first number. It was to recover "the distinctive outlook of the Christian faith and tradition" along Anglo-Catholic lines. The LKG had established the quarterly, its readers were informed, "to present and elaborate a Catholic view of social issues and the construction of a valid alternative to the pagan developments of contemporary Plutocracy." Temple, in his foreward, alluded to those who think there should be no relationship between religion and sociology. They are wrong. Wrong, too, are those who want us to "deduce economic laws of the ideal society from the Gospel and then either gradually or abruptly to conform our behavior to those laws." In typical Temple fashion, he said that there were numerous intermediaries between these two extremes. But in a decade in which the country would eventually and clumsily find its way to the "middle way" *Christendom* was in no mood for compromise. Indeed, in its solid and sometimes truculent Anglo-Catholicism, it was critical not only of pagan plutocracy but also of Christian progressives for whom "the Kingdom of God and the transcendent claims of the Christian revelation may be equated with a zeal for 'social righteousness' expressed through an undenominationalism scarcely distinguishable from a secular reforming enthusiasm."

The Christendom Group always had American connections, principally through Joseph Fletcher (of later situation ethics fame) and this connection was documented in the premier issue of the journal. V. A. Demant, in an article titled "The Prospects of Christian Sociology in America," mentioned his meetings with the executive board of the Civil Liberties Union and with the (Episcopal) Church League for Industrial Democracy in New York. His closest colleague in the U. S, was Prof. Frank Gavin, who occasionally wrote for *Christendom*. Another was Prof. Vida Scudder, who worked on an American version of the Summer School of Sociology. Demant assessed social Christian efforts in this country as "unofficial, minor and sporadic," but he thought that, in general, the churches were becoming more widely and deeply concerned with social problems. Demant was bothered by what he regarded as a diminished appreciation for sin and a consequent "can do" optimism among U. S. Social gospelers. And he pointed in particular to the need for a focus on the "game of finance" which became almost an obsession for Demant and others. There is much ambulance-type social service going on, he noted, but he also wondered whether its general acceptance would blunt calls for fundamental changes in social structure.

Demant was reading Walter Lippmann at this time as was Widdrington, who wrote in the first issue on "The Coming of the Leisure State," a topic to which he would return a number of times in the thirties and on which he was in advance of his epoch.

Already in the second issue (June, 1931), the Thomistic cast of the journal is clearly visible. Ruth Kenyon wrote on the Schoolmen, Reckitt penned a very favorable review of Jacques Maritain's *The Things That Are Not Caesar's* and Demant recommended Christopher Dawson's *Progress and Religion*. Maritain and Dawson became special *Christendom* favorites as did Nicolas Berdyaev, from the Orthodox side, who appeared in the December, 1931 number.[22] The trademark *Christendom* theme of financial skullduggery in high places also emerged clearly and not only in the person of Demant. Reckitt wrote that finance was openly warring against civilization, an accusation repeated by W. T. Symons. Neither had a clue as to what the church should do about it.

A fitting commentary on the *Christendom* enterprise, although not written specifically in response to it, came in the form of Oliver Quick's 1931 book *Philosophy and the Cross*. He did not reject scholasticism out of hand. It urges on us, he wrote, a catholicity of thought which is sometimes lost sight of in an era of theological specialization. And he appreciated the powerful attraction of authority and infallibility in a time of bewildering contrariness. Yet to become unbewildered by embracing this or that absolutism, Quick warned, is to contravene the Law of the cross, which says that we must relinquish a lower order of truth to grasp a higher. Quick's question: Are we willing to give up preconceived notions of how the world must be and "go to school with the world?" This kind of theological modesty was, for Quick, the true *amor intellectualis Dei*.[23] It was a modesty the *Christendom* crowd had some difficulty in demonstrating.

The major focus of peoples' attention in 1931 was the fragile economy; yet the Upper House of York Convocation found time to discuss gambling, interest in which rose throughout the interwar years. The convocators judged it to be a "grave, prolific source of evil" and declared themselves against it.[24] Widespread as the phenomenon was, it was a low priority for church discussions generally, Canon Peter Green being virtually alone in according it serious, sustained attention.[25] For millions, the trip to the betting parlor or the greyhound track was becoming a normal part of life; for the unemployed, it was a way to relieve boredom. Gaming, along with sports, was part of an emerging culture, abetted by radio, cinema and the press, that knitted together a nation that found itself, at the 1931 watershed, in a "frightened and irritable mood."[26]

The most significant event for social Christianity, on the immediate other side of the watershed, was the death of Charles Gore in 1932. In a history of the Christian social movement published that same year, Maurice Reckitt wrote that Gore was "the acknowledged father of the post-war movement."[27] He was, indeed, the commanding figure, not only in his own Anglo-Catholic wing and not only in the application of religion to society but throughout the English Church and in several fields of endeavor. His writing on foundational theology was the principal *vademecum* for generations of theological students; more than anyone else, he was responsible for a Maurician, creation-centered, incarnational theology's becoming firmly embedded in Anglican thinking. That incarnational theology, which would not allow spirit to be split off from matter, served as a natural context for bring together commitment to the eschatological Kingdom and concern for the temporal order. Anglican social thought went off in a number of directions and was far from univocal. But it owed to Gore a steadiness, a rooting in biblical theology, that gave it integrity and, as John Orens has written, saved it from confusing "the word of the Lord with mere trendiness."[28] He taught his contemporaries to think comprehensively: to relate critical biblical scholarship, not reflexively to itself, but to the larger life of the church; to relate doctrine, not just to the life of the individual believer, but to society as the arena of divine activity; and to relate one's own ecclesial family to others in the *oikumene*. His death was by no means the end of his influence. His liberal catholic impulses continued to animate William Temple and, through him, global Christianity.

The quest for catholic comprehensiveness appears in Temple's Gifford Lectures, begun in 1932 and published as *Nature, Man and God* two years later. While modern philosophy was abandoning any synthetic pretensions, Temple held to the classical tradition in which philosophy is the dialectical companion to theology, which was logically if not operationally queen of the sciences. But Temple's greatness is shown by the fact that, contrary to some of his contemporaries, he was not led by his synthetic urge to escape the dialectic by embracing the Grand Scheme. He acknowledged that there was a new appreciation abroad for a medieval Christendom styled by Hobbes as "the ghost of the deceased Roman Empire, sitting crowned upon the grave thereof." Yet "the antithesis of Luther and Descartes has so shattered the thesis of Hildebrand and Aquinas that it cannot be re-established."[29] With the antitheses also "moribund," we are compelled to look for a synthesis in order-with-liberty. For Temple, this would entail a world federal structure of government inculcating a universal civilization.[30] In the moral arena it would mean a "commonwealth of value." Here again, Temple displays greatness. While other Christian thinkers were calling for the recreation of a Christian order as the single way out of the "modern welter," Temple, although he recognized that the faithful would call the commonwealth of value the Communion of Saints, argued for a world order independent of sectarian theological categories. If some longed to be citizens of Christendom, Temple, still the gospel apologist, was comfortable as a citizen of the world.[31]

That world, according to *Christendom* editor Widdrington was, in 1932, "cast loose from its moorings and is engaged in an adventure in which no one can see the end."[32] This end-of-an-epoch atmosphere of crisis and collapse pervaded the journal throughout the thirties. It took notice of world event but it was less interested in political commentary than in broad cultural analysis and in defining "the task of Christian sociology." It did acknowledge some dissension in its ranks on the question of the best way to approach that task. Some were inclined toward an activist stance, joining, e.g., members of the LKG (and other non-member clergy) in publicly protesting the Means Test. Others, in the majority, viewed their special vocation as thinking through a systematic social philosophy based on Christian dogma and on the moral tradition of catholicism. This gave rise to charges of intellectual isolation and a reliance on jargon, reflected in its pages already in 1932 as it defended its intention, following Maurice, to dig and not to plant. Curiously, with all its donnishness, the *Christendom* cadre also displayed a streak of anti-intellectualism to the degree that it refused to live in the hard world of fact and politically possibility. Classicist Edwyn Bevan commented on this phenomenon in 1932, although without direct reference to *Christendom*. He traced interest in the Middle Ages to the romantic movement which got its start in the early nineteenth century and noted a strain of it in Neville Figgis and in Newman's "illative sense."[33] The romantic spirit of the grand gesture and the golden age found congenial shelter in many places, including in the Ruskin-Morris tradition and in various socialisms, and it was able to tarry comfortably also in *Christendom*.

This is not to say that there was no fine, sharp thinking in the journal. There was much and much fine writing, too. But *Christendom* was part of an era the participants in which often felt helpless, their attempts at intellectual construction knocked cockeyed by the rush of events. And for some, the temptation to turn to the past for fixed points, for a center that held, was irresistible.

An especially blatant form of this romanticism was the "back to the land" movement. Already in 1843 the northern radical Feargus O'Connor put forward a social scheme along ruralist lines[34] and many, following Blake and, later, Morris in regarding machines and mills as dark and satanic, were inclined to beat a retreat to the happy village. They were known in this period as distributists, men like Chesterton and Belloc who were extremely critical not only of advancing industrialism but also of centralization or state socialism.

Another important figure in the ruralist movement was Eric Gill, a sculptor who, in his early years, shared with what Stanley Pierson calls "aesthetically oriented Socialists" the idea that trade unions and the Labour Party should join forces to struggle against commercialism.[35] Over the years, however, he lost faith in that idea and in Fabian-type legislation to solve deep-seated problems. Spurning politics, he turned to religion, regarding the artist as the *vox Dei*; he entered the Roman Church in 1913. He founded a Roman Catholic artistic colony at Ditchling and was also the force behind the Guild of St. Joseph and St. Dominic. In 1924 he moved the colony to an old Benedictine monastery in Wales and, long before the environmentalist and ecology movements flourished (trivium: "environment" is a neologism by Carlyle in *Sartor Resartus*) attempted to live in a pre-industrial way, close to the land and in harmony with the rhythms of nature. He returned to England, to Buckinghamshire, in 1928 and died in 1940. Writing with admirable clarity and simplicity, Gill made his anti-capitalist Christian apologetic accessible to the reading public in *Christianity and the Machine Age* (1940) and in *In a Strange Land* (1944).

In addition to A. J. Penty, whom I have mentioned, another ruralist leader was the flamboyant Fr. Vincent McNabb. He made his case for an exodus from the city to the countryside in a witty, breezy, engaging literary style, in *Nazareth or Social Chaos?* in 1933. Nazareth, or the village of manageable scale, was the basic unit of society when sanity and catholic order prevailed: in the Middle Ages. Only a recreated peasantry established on its own land could save civilization. These ideas were advanced by

McNabb and others in the quarterly *Land for the People* and in a 1934 book, *Flee to the Fields*, a quotation from which gives a flavor of its author's mind set: "Brittany or provincial France or Rhineland Germany or Basque-land represent normal and right human life, and Birmingham or Belfast or Berlin or Chicago an abnormal and perilous departure from it."[36]

It would be hard to find a group (the ruralists) in which the elements of medieval nostalgia, Luddism, romanticism and neo-Thomism were displayed in more vivid, almost cartoonish ways. It was true that Copec had called for the revitalizing of rural life following the depradations of war, the industrial revolution and the general encroachment of urban life. It was also true that there was a "leisure boom" during the thirties which included a rediscovery of the countryside on hikes and bicycle excursions. But if not everyone was prepared to heed Stephen Spender's invitation "Come, let us praise the gas-works," Britain's future was firmly in the cities, from which few would follow the distributists in what Sidney Dark called, sardonically, their "happy retrogression."

Mainstream views on Britain's contemporary problems were offered by a veritable parade of Christian social thinkers in a collection of essays, *Christianity and the Crisis*, edited by Percy Dearmer. The fearful mood of the times was caught by the volume's title and in Dearmer's introduction: national life stands in dire need of moralizing, as it did after Waterloo in 1815. The moral aspect of money is overlooked; the situation is almost out of hand; we are on the brink of disaster at home and abroad. And out of a mosaic of metaphors came a tangle of solutions. Dearmer asserted that only Christ could save the world from ruin, but neglected to say how that would be accomplished, blandly and facilely defining Christianity as "the religion of all good men."[37] He also suggested that international federalism was the correct political solution to the crisis.

Interestingly, the very muddle represented by the book is alluded to in the volume itself in one of its most perceptive papers. W. R. Matthews, Dean of Exeter, saw no dominant trend in intellectual life and "in this incoherence of modern knowledge and thought...lies the essence of the crisis."[38] Advances in physics and psychology have bequeathed no integrated picture either of the universe or of humanity, he suggested. Pragmatism, with its distrust of systems, has abetted, if not sponsored, a revolt against reason. All around, Matthews glimpsed the "despair of finding any fixed and eternal standpoint, or even the joyous recognition that such fixed standpoints are unnecessary." Hence the words, strewn about the volume and era: mess, deadlock, confusion, chaos, disaster. In the church, he wrote, are reflected the two main intellectual currents outside it: return to reason (A. E. Taylor, Temple) and distrust of reason (R. Otto). Matthews failed to develop his typology fully, however; in its neo-Thomism and romanticism, *Christendom* could be seen to accommodate elements of both.

P. T. R. Kirk contributed one of the worst essays. He included a diatribe against economist, precisely the people he and his colleagues should have been listening to, and delivered himself of sweeping judgments: "Banking is...in control of men whose mentality is divorced from questions of human need."[39] And again, the only choice was "Christ or Anti-Christ." Some of the papers were routine, like Temple's, breaking no new ground but in the aggregate they demonstrate that the ecumenical church was far from knowing its own mind on social and economic questions in 1933. Yet the nation as a whole was no more unified in direction and Christian social thinkers were making their contribution, however gropingly, to a type of thinking that would welcome solutions, when they finally came down the "middle way," to at least some of the "mess" they faced.[40]

The mess was not only domestic but international in scope. Unemployment stood at 3 million in 1933, highest in the interwar years, but severe economic stress was affecting every society except Russia's; it did not have an advanced economy. Due partly to this stress, Hitler came to power in a "new" Germany and Reckitt, writing in *Christendom*, saw disaster impending: "Everything points to the tragic possibility that in half a dozen years' time modern youth may have to face the moral dilemmas which tortured the consciences of their fathers.[41] The journal was also aware of the *Kirchenkampf* under Nazi pressure and Ruth Kenyon scored the "German Christians" for their supineness. The Jewish question was discussed little, although the existence of concentration camps was known.

Christendom was concerned, in 1933, with the continental liturgical revival, of which it approved; with Barthianism, about which it had some good things to say; and with the Oxford Group Movement, or Buchmanism, which was received with favor by few among social Christians.[42] Socialism was also a concern, with perpetual gadfly Robert Woodifield writing to complain of *Christendom*'s distancing itself from socialism and with anti-collectivist Reckitt replying that it leads to tyranny and that its moral motor was running down. And along with everyone else, the journal was tracing the adumbrations of social Christianity in the Oxford Movement, the centenary of which was celebrated in 1933. The major focus that year, however, for the LKG and the journal, was the international arena. The ninth Summer School of Sociology featured Eliot, Berdyaev, Gillett and Rosenthal speaking on "Catholicism and International Order." They saw the secular order disintegrating around them but were hard put to come up with concrete actions Christians could take. It was thought that the League of Nations was "worth preserving," but the main emphasis was on the creation of a "Catholic world-order;" the way to that order was never, however, made clear.

Kenyon's comment was apt: "We have not yet, in our reviving Christian sociology, a clear doctrine of Christian Politics in a world not accepting Christianity."[43]

There was little doubt in the minds of at least some members of the LKG that when a "clear doctrine" would surface, it would do so precisely in the LKG. W. G. Peck, lecturing to an American audience at Seabury-Western Seminary, let it be known that the LKG was heir to the best of the Tractarian tradition, font of all true reform in the English Church.[44] The Tractarians did help the church rethink its relationship to its own theological tradition and to society and in this and in other ways it contributed to the appearance (or re-appearance) of a socially-aware Christianity. Yet Peck was so opposed, as were the Tractarians, to a purely instrumental understanding of the church, that he commended its complete disengagement from plans for social reform of secular provenance...a note struck also by Reckitt in his rejoinder to Woodifield. Indeed, Peck did not hesitate to speak of "the ethico-social sovereignty of the Church as the Divine Society."[45] And in the either/or mode of the times, he warned that "the alternative before mankind is the reformulation of civilization around a resurgent Christian Church, or a human chaos of which the dark possibilities are endless."[46] It was this sort of thinking or, better, rhetoric, that contributed greatly to the marginalizing of social Christianity in some of its expressions and elicited Alec Vidler's rueful observation, "They meant well, but to mean well is never enough."[47]

The international focus of the LKG was shared by Temple in his address to the York Diocesan Conference in June, 1933. The Marxist writer John Strachey's book *The Coming Struggle for Power*, brought out the previous year, had helped produce, according to Julian Symons, a whole new outlook, at least on the left, which regarded members of the working class as possessors of great virtue and saw many positive values in Soviet society.[48] And the Archbishop's thinking seemed to move in a similar direction: Communists were working, he told his clergy, for a social order based on unselfish cooperation and he urged them not to underestimate the remarkable achievements wrought by heretofore unskilled peasants in industry. But as for communism as an ideology: it is "the most severe menace which has threatened the Christian faith in the civilized world for

some hundreds of years."[49] His argument was simple. Communism rules
out God, who transcends the state and from whom persons derive their
integrity and freedom; and, said Temple, echoing his mentor, Gore, private
property is an expression of this freedom. Yet Temple prudently warned
against an anti-communist campaign that would only give it free publicity.
The way to combat it is to be critics of one's own social order, in which
many are propertyless. The final aim of economic reform is the elimination
of an oppressed proletariat, thus undercutting communism's appeal for
revolution.

     To many, the situation was desperate both at home and abroad.
Unemployment was massive and the masses in several countries were
turning to fascism. It is therefore not surprising that, as Joseph Needham
observed, "by 1933 the general movement among all kinds of intellectual
workers in England towards political activity was becoming widespread."[50]
For social Christians, however, it was the end of an era of activism and
prophetism, of wondering whether or not this socialism or that party
platform crystallized the aims of the Kingdom of God. Social Christians
were entering a new period of theological reflection, of social and economic
research that would eventually find expression, no longer in the "little
societies" or in heroic figures but in the careful constructions of the Life and
Work movement and, later, of the World Council of Churches. Left behind
would be the grammar of evolutionary optimism: "I was still talking like
that," admitted a chastened Temple, "when Hitler became Chancellor of the
German Reich."[51]

     "We renounce war and never again, directly or indirectly, will we support
or sanction another." In a letter to the press on October 16, 1933, the
mercurial Dick Sheppard had asked members of the public to write that
provocative sentence on a postcard and send it to him. He got 100,000
replies. Gentle and whimsical, out of place as Dean of Canterbury, even
more so as Canon of St. Paul's but "the most truly religious man of his
generation," according to Sidney Dark,[52] Sheppard was also one of the most
nationally visible Anglican clerics in the interwar years. He virtually
invented religious broadcasting as vicar of St. Martin-in-the-Fields and was
an enthusiastic evangelist but in the middle thirties he began to be obsessed
with the fear of war and devoted his energies almost exclusively to pacifist
causes.

     As was shown by the strikingly large response to his postcard appeal,
Sheppard was far from alone in his dread of another 1914 or in his activist
determination not to stand idly by while the world went off to war. In
February of the previous year, the Oxford Union had scandalized

traditionalists by passing a resolution declaring "that this House will in no circumstances fight for its king and country," a sentiment that was seconded by numbers of working class organizations as well. This movement of students in a body to the left was something new but, as should be obvious from the present study, the confecting of leagues, unions, guilds, etc. was not. Thus Sheppard, responding to this broad anti-war feeling, formed the Peace Pledge Union, which was joined by pacifists and by those not strictly in the pacifist camp; it included prominent Christians like Donald Soper (a leading figure in Christian Socialism after World War II), Eric Gill and George Lansbury.

Sheppard was also behind the Peace Ballot. Conducted during 1934 and 1935, it was called the Ballot of Blood by the conservative press and was the occasion of a great deal of debate throughout the country. It became more than a mere sampling of opinion; it became a crusade, the most massive effort of its kind up to that time (much of it organized by women) and, in the end, more people filled out a Peace Ballot than voted in the general election. The result: support for the League of Nations, arms reduction and a collective stand against aggression. The Ballot reflected a division shaping up in the nation, between those, led by leftist intellectuals, who had a sharp sense of the evils of fascism and those, represented by the upper-echelon Cliveden Set, who were convinced that peace lay on the path of appeasement.

Christendom offered pale support for the Peace Ballot but reminded its readers that the question of peace is finally one of international order, not simply of stop-gap measures like arms reduction. It also reprinted the Pastoral Letter on Peace and War, issued in November, 1934 by the bishops of the American Episcopal Church, a document that attacked what we now call the arms race as conducive to war. The journal noted the first Anglo-Catholic School of Sociology, held in September, 1934 near Boston, with the Bishop of Maine presiding. Visitor W. G. Peck cited the dominance of clergy at the School but was pleased at the passion for social justice participants evinced; at Oxford, he said, there is "sometimes more light than warmth.[53] He also was impressed, although not favorably, by the Americans' pragmatic spirit: they want to move quickly from analysis to action, he remarked. In general, *Christendom* was scornful of activism. Kenyon argued that the Church Union, which made the Summer School at Oxford an official part of its structure in 934, needed to say what Christian sociology *is* before it could be "applied." The journal disliked Roosevelt...his *On Our Way* Peck found "dull and superficial"...and criticized the New Deal as an exercise in trial and error, rather than representing a coherent social philosophy.[54]

Peck was also critical of the Americans for not taking communism as a philosophy seriously. This was not the case with their British cousins. The 1934 Summer School focussed on "Communism and its Rivals" and featured a "tense duel" between Julius Hecker and Berdyaev. Christopher Dawson's lecture, reprinted in the journal, was a careful, profound analysis of Marx's "social apocalyptic," which Dawson regarded as a secularized appropriation of biblical apocalyptic.   Still, the overall project of *Christendom*, the search for an autochthonous (actually, Archimedean) Christian standpoint, was stated forcefully by Reckitt: the journal is not against communism only, but against capitalism and "the whole modern world of avarice and power" which leads to nationalist fanaticism. Indeed, Reckitt seems to have been the chief reason why the journal felt compelled to issue those recurring disclaimers that it advocated backward-looking nostalgia.[55]

I have given much attention to efforts at developing a comprehensive social philosophy, especially within Anglo-Catholic circles. It is well to remember, however, that not everyone was enthusiastic about the project nor about the way the Christendom Group went about it. For example, Wilfred Knox, one of liberal Anglo-Catholicism's most gifted and subtle leaders, complained of the lack of viable models in 1934, referring offhandedly to Reckitt's "attempt."[56] Communism was out of the question, distributism attractive but impractical and socialism, "as a political movement, is not very sure of itself," he thought.[57] And Lord Hugh Cecil commented that many were wasting their time on trivia, on liturgical and devotional "silliness" instead of attending to the serious issues of the day.[58] Among Christians and among the general populace the feeling was abroad that a way out of the dangerous confusion of their world had to be found; only a comparative few thought that way would lead through the church's dogmatic tradition.

Both Houses of Canterbury Convocation spent a good deal of time struggling with the issue of unemployment in 1933-34, with the debate reflecting the confusion of thought in the country. The Upper House was treated to a more-opinionated-than-sensible tirade against the Industrial Christian Fellowship's efforts on behalf of the unemployed by A. C. Headlam, but the bishops managed to pass only a mild resolution of concern.[59] The convocators, with the rest of the nation, expressed great worry about the pitiful failure of the Disarmament Conference - it served many at the time as a focus for their fear of coming war - and about worsening relations between church and state in Germany. The continuing problem of inadequate and scarce housing was also on their minds and was the subject of an appeal for slum clearance funds issued by the two Archbishops in 1934.

The response of the Church Union (a merger of the English Church Union and the Anglo-Catholic Congress) was to form a Housing Association, which was instrumental in creating Public Utility Societies in several urban areas. The Association also began a magazine, *Church and Slum*, in 1934. Its lead number contained Archiepiscopal endorsement, the by now requisite reference to Weston's tabernacle/slum speech and the declaration "Money, Bricks and Mortar Themselves Become Sacramental." In its theological rationale for the Anglican Church's involvement in clearing and building, a favorite theme of Christian social thinkers was highlighted: the deleterious moral effect of degrading environmental conditions, a theme with deep roots in the Platonic heritage. "It is unreasonable to expect nobility of character to spring out of a hovel." Gore, too, was invoked as was a familiar strand in his theology: "Catholics must work for the improvement of housing because they believe in the Incarnation."[60] The magazine supported the Greenwood Act which, however, had resulted chiefly in slum clearance, not rebuilding, and it was not reluctant to call for action on the part of the central government. It argued for a National Housing Corporation (it also called it a Board) without neglecting to urge the Church to get its own house in order. In the tradition of Octavia Hill it reminded the Church that a landlord is more than a rent collector but has moral obligations to the tenants and noted with approval the resolve of the Ecclesiastical Commission to spend Ł 1 million over a four year period for rehousing.

The Church in 1934 was able, with the nation at large, to do little in the face of economic distress and international tension; but in an England where too many towns in addition to Jarrow were "a perpetual penniless bleak Sabbath,"[61] it could attempt to make the lives of some of J. B. Priestley's factory girls-looking-like-actresses less wretched.

Women in the Church of England appeared on the agenda the following year with the issuing of the Report of the Archbishops' Commission on the Ministry of Women. Noting that their freedom and status had advanced in the Church and in secular society since the 1919 Ministry of Women document, the Report reflected continuing uncertainty about the position of deaconesses and their leading worship in consecrated buildings. It called for more "semi-professional" female works in the Church[62] but stopped short of recommending their admission to the priesthood. The Report did contain a qualifying codicil, however, written by W. R. Matthews, which stated that arguments the Report presented in support of its position on an all-male priesthood were without value.[63] (The year 1935 also saw the publication of another Report, from the Commission on Church and State).

While the Church of England as a body was absorbed with matters internal, its members were busy with their search for social remedies. This search, which, as I have been trying to show, transcended a mere and superficial "social gospel," could be well traced in a mid-decade volume, *Faith That Illuminates*; it contained lectures by Eliot, Widdrington, Peck, Reckitt, Slesser and R. Ellis Roberts, given at St. John-the-Divine, Richmond, Surrey and edited by its vicar, Demant. In it, he labeled collectivism "heresy" and wanted to see Barth's theology of crisis and Maritain's neo-Scholasticism as the only vital movements of his day. They both were able to formulate a useful anthropology, a false rendering of which lay at the heart, for Demant, of society's malaise.[64]

Widdrington's theme was the proper use of leisure in the Power Age while Peck, mentioning other religions but using them only as a foil for Christianity, argued that only the Christian faith in its catholic form "will guide us out of the chaotic welter in which we are now struggling."[65] The emerging "Christian Eliot" viewed the whole of modern literature as having been corrupted by secularism and Roberts and Slesser joined Peck in extolling Christian dogma, the latter emphasizing its Thomistic form. The entire volume reveals how desperate important Christian thinkers were and how narrow and unaccommodating that desperation made them.

A certain jittery ardor, if not desperation, seems to be reflected in Hewlett Johnson's Social Credit pamphlet of 1935. He was sure that the "National Discount" would "save us from the menace of an acquisitive society" and win the "war on poverty."[66] Douglas was also being recommended to the York Diocesan Clergy School by Reckitt[67] as well as to a general audience by Edwin Muir.[68] And, in a "worst case scenario," it was being touted by a Coventry vicar, one Robert J. Scrutton, as a panacea: it would achieve the medieval Just Price, free politics from "all sordid elements," wipe out crime, give all a short work week, eliminate unemployment, class conflict and war.[69] Milder approval of Douglas was conferred by Cyril E. Hudson, Canon of St. Albans and a Reckitt associate, whose book, *Preface to a Christian Sociology* presented many of the points made by *Christendom*. "It is hardly possible to exaggerate," he wrote in 1935, "the prevalence of the mood of impotence and despair at the present day."[70]

If many were feeling impotent and despairing, others were gaining at least some slight hopeful energy from the economic recovery mentioned at the beginning of this chapter, "despaired of in 1931, in the air by 1933, obvious

by 1935."[71] Planning, too, said *The Economist*,[72] was in the air and the
authors of *Christianity and the Social Revolution* were speculating on the
contribution religion would make to the revision of Britain.   Their
speculation took the form of finding common ground between communist
and Christian idealism, seeing in it the impetus toward a New Order. C. E.
Raven called communism "a new apocalyptic" and praised both the
idealism of the Russian experiment and the enthusiasm and commitment of
British communists; they are not rigid, monolithic,[73] W. H. Auden added,
in a rambling, loose essay, "The Good Life."

Ever fast on the alliterative draw, Conrad Noel wrote of "Christ the
Communist" and the apocalyptically-induced New Order he came to
announce: the essay would persuade only the already convinced. Similarly,
John Lewis spoke of "Christ the Socialist" and his apocalyptic, thus
revolutionary, thus Marxian views.   "The new Christ," he wrote
breathlessly, "is the insurgent Proletariat" to which the church must accord
reverence.[74] In a paper of indifferent quality, R. Pascal styled all past
peasant uprisings and monastic movements communistic, while Joseph
Needham saw his contemporaries standing "at the turning point between
two civilizations," the one, individualistic, the other, collectivist. The
capitalist system, he was sure, would be overthrown.

Clive Binyon's contribution is instructive. He began a short history of
Christian socialism with Hardie, Lansbury and Snowden, remarking that
their political positions have a moral but only a generally Christian basis.
This kind of diffuse, non-kerygmatic Christianity can be damaging to the
church: in forgetting the Fall and Judgment, an immanental theology shades
over into pantheism. Here Binyon put his finger on a problem in social
Christianity that was often overlooked. Just as, for Binyon, "social" and
"socialist" are interchangeable, so, in Christian discourse, "moral" and
"Christian" come to be synonymous. This is a complex matter in the
context of a society which, on the one hand, has an established church and
a Christian heritage and, on the other, is moving toward a pluralist future in
the nineties. The lack of attention to it is seen most vividly in the
Christendom Group. Its members' need to hammer out Christian
distinctives led them to draw into themselves, drawing a radical distinction
between a sharply-defined Christian civilization and the flawed work as
they found it. Perhaps the ferociousness of their response could have been
modulated, usefully, had the particular/universal tension been more fully
addressed.

Binyon included comments on the general shape of social Christianity in
1935. The Industrial Christian Fellowship, he said, met with an initially

tepid reception from many socially aware Christians but now, under P. T. R. Kirk, it is "one of the really live elements in the Christian Socialist Movement."[75]   Copec gave the movement a "new start" and supplied impetus to the Christian Social Council, the most significant component of which, he felt, was the research department. And his harsh judgment of the Socialist Christian League and the Catholic Crusade: they want to influence the world without caring what the church thinks.

The volume's worst essay, an almost hysterical one, was by John Cornford.   Eventually, he thought, the church would unite against revolutionary communism; the two are completely incompatible, but right is on the communist side. Needham, however, in a second essay, pointed out that the hatred of oppression and a strict morality at the heart of communism were nurtured in a Christian civilization. And in one of the most lucid papers, Reinhold Niebuhr treated communism *as* a religion. In sum, the volume as a whole speaks volumes about the disarray in which the Christian left found itself in 1935. That disarray was the case with the rest of social Christianity as it was with the British intelligentsia generally.[76]

We find the Anglo-Catholic barrister Kenneth Ingram agreeing with Needham in *The Coming Civilization*. He offered his usual analysis of the imminent collapse of capitalism, evidence for which he claimed to have found in, *inter alia*, Lippmann, Auden, Spender and Huxley; he looked to Russia, with all its admitted problems, as something of a model for the new world aborning. The apologetic theme is prominent. The church, he wrote, presents itself to the popular mind as existing in a mental backwater. It must show that it can posit, promote and be the nucleus for the coming Christian civilization (the opposite of materialist civilization in Ingram's system) in order to win back the alienated. Those among that throng who retained their critical faculties and sense of history might have been confirmed, however, in their alienation upon reading a characteristic Ingram teaser like "Is Christianity being reborn in so unlikely a Bethlehem as Russian Communism?"[77]

Economic reconstruction was on the minds of the eighty participants in a three-day conference, held in 1935, of the ecumenical Christian Social Council. The situation, they felt, was precarious, with economic events outstripping people's ability to come up with political solutions. Self-interest, rather than the motive of service was driving the economy, causing workers to be subordinated to the needs of production. Class strife abounded. And the financial interests, they thought, wielded unwarranted power. These and other social Christian commonplaces were summarized by Malcolm Spencer in *Economics and God*, a kind of textbook and compendium of mainstream thought of the mid-thirties. Spencer, much influenced by A. D. Lindsay, was afraid of the move toward collectivism he detected in the country, fearful of its liberty-depriving potential. He took a favorable view of government economic planning, however, but wanted the government to encourage small industries and pursue a policy of decentralization. The government should also underwrite the security of the poor and conduct more bold experiments for the relief of unemployment. Spencer was refreshing in his reliance on the empirical method and refreshing, too, in his flexibility of mind: in his book he repudiated his earlier defense of Dougal in his 1932 *Building on Sand*. It is, he wrote of Social Credit, "technically wrong."[78] Representing much of the thinking going on at the time, Spencer placed large emphasis on banking and finance and, as he heard the government announce the most significant peacetime increase in arms expenditure and observed the international scramble for markets, he worried about war.

The Archbishop of Canterbury told Canterbury Convocation of his view of the international situation in June, 1935, terming it "ominous" but finding grounds for hope in a recent speech by Hitler. He felt that Germany should be allowed to take its rightful place again as an equal among the nations, although he acknowledged that the religious atmosphere there was not good. His support of the League of Nations was solid.

For Temple, the dominant issue in 1935 was the question of peace or war.[79] He thought that what was needed was criticism of an unchristian nationalism which regards other nations only as potential enemies. The principle of world-fellowship requires all states to accept arbitration and end competition in acquiring arms. He joined the Primate in supporting the League but warned that it was impotent without a firm commitment to collective security.

Temple made his second visit to the United States in 1935, addressing the Student Christian Movement in Indianapolis. In November, the same month in which the so-called National Government was returned with a large Tory majority, Temple convoked what was essentially a huge pep rally for social Christians - a Copec pick-me-up - which overflowed the Albert Hall. In an atmosphere charged with great fervor, attenders pledged, at Temple's invitation, to take their enthusiasm for social righteousness back to their parishes, to fight against the evils like unemployment and the exploitive treatment of the employed. It was the case that many in those parishes still needed to be convinced that Christian teaching was salient outside the "spiritual" sphere. It was also the case that the potential of the parishes as agents of social renewal was an underdeveloped theme in the interwar period.

Christendom voiced its enthusiasm for the Albert Hall rally and the participants' commitment to action. This stood in contrast, the journal felt, to Baldwin's pessimistic acceptance of unemployment as permanent. Yet in reading the pages of the journal parishioners would be treated to few practical suggestions for making their social passion practical. In fact, its own enthusiasm for moralizing the social order seems to have flagged somewhat under the pressure of events abroad. The chief threats to the faith were located in Moscow and Berlin, Reckitt believed, and he recommended a strategic retreat back to foundational theology. And one of the solid contributions the journal made, in fact, was theological rather than sociological: especially in the person of Widdrington, it lifted up the need for a theology of technology and of a leisure culture, the need for which continues to be felt in our day of smart machines, automated factories and the Internet. In 1935, e.g., Widdrington was struggling with Lewis Mumford's *Technic and Civilization*. His other great passion at this time, as has been mentioned, was aiding the 180,000 Russian exiles living in Paris and he issued a plea for readers to join him in that work by sending contributions. Here, at least, was something definite to do!

Christendom was perhaps the single most powerful force in social Christian circles in the thirties but it was not without its critics, as I have indicated.[80] Criticism of its medievalism was reflected in the March, 1935 issue, in which Demant spiritedly responded to "a recent students' conference [which] took care to include among its resolutions a warning to Christians against looking to Medieval thought for social guidance and against adopting a particular economic theory." He defended the medieval order as one directed toward truly human ends. But his disclaimer...that he is not arguing for a return of the medieval social structure...was simply asserted and is unconvincing. Clarity of social purpose was not a legacy left to Christendom by *Christendom*.

Controversy was not limited to student conferences. The pages of the *Green Quarterly* crackled with it in the mid-thirties, beginning with W. L. Knox's comments on writing by Demant, Lindsay and Peck. Demant and Peck, he suggested, overstate present difficulties, entertain unrealistic views of the Middle Ages and falsely assume that catholic dogma leads ineluctably to a new economic system.[81] Knox's arguments seem to prefigure those raised later against evangelical apologist Francis Schaefer: these gentlemen do not take the complexity of history with sufficient seriousness; it simply will not do to regard Renaissance humanism and Kant as wholly evil. Lindsay (whom Knox liked) in fact appeals to Kant to support the idea of

Christianizing the economic order. Nor was there much social justice or individual liberty in the Middle Ages, wrote Knox in the strongest condemnation of interwar medievalism I ran across in the literature. For Knox, Lindsay was superior precisely because he avoided indulging in romantic utopias.

The next issue carried Demant's reply. He rejected Kant because the latter sundered morals from metaphysics; he was, therefore, Protestant, the utility epithet typically hurled by Anglo-Catholics at anyone or anything they happened not to like. "Medievalists" are imaginary creatures, he contended and all Demant and *Christendom* derive from the Schoolmen is a personal and social teleology and certainly no economic system. Yet he went on to say that catholic philosophy is the *sole* one that puts everything in proper balance.[82]

The debate continued in later issues, reflecting an emotionally charged atmosphere - this was no mere academic altercation - and demonstrating the difficulty of finding common definitions for words like "liberty," "medieval" and "economic system."

The *Quarterly* paid attention to matters economic in 1935 with an article on the Church Assembly's debate on unemployment, noting the prominence of Douglasite arguments. It (now the *New Green Quarterly*) noted a division between those who would offer a definite economic policy emanating from the church and those who would bless (or condemn) policies already at hand. The *Quarterly* leaned in the latter direction, glad that there was no church parliamentary party. It was also paying increased heed to issues of peace and war, pausing to comment on the coming of television and its possible use in evangelism. Its small notice of the death of Basil Jellicoe (a "real enthusiast") was not indicative of his later fame.

Amid all the talk of war in 1935, what has been described as the "outstanding social change" in the period was quietly taking place: the growth of the "white collar" sector of the workforce.[83] And suburbia was growing with them, sprawling, planless, despite the Restriction of Ribbon Development Act of 1935. "All over everywhere little houses were erupting like pimples"[84] across what poet Anne Fremantle called "the country's smug, suburban face."[85]

Suburbanites and others on the higher end of the economic scale, especially if they lived in the south, were relatively well off. People were taking advantage of the new hire-purchase schemes to fill their bedrooms and parlors with amply-upholstered "sets." They were staying home more, playing Mah Jong, the American import, and doing their daily crossword puzzle, wildly popular in the thirties. They were also increasing their consumption of printed materials, including novels and mysteries. When they did go out, it was likely to listen and dance to American popular music, or to attend the cinema; plush theater palaces were mushrooming across the country, crowding out the old music halls and contributing their share to a certain "Americanization" of culture that would escalate considerably after World War II. Large, well-appointed coaches began to ply the roads, inciting J. B. Priestley to remark that if one had a little money one could "live the life of a satrap." In fact, Baldwin had confidently announced in 1936 that Britain had left "Bleak House" and entered "Great Expectations;" and it was indeed the case that standards of living for everyone were rising throughout the thirties, due little to actions the government took or did not take.

The picture was a good deal less sanguine for people on the bottom. Sir John Boyd Orr canvassed the country in 1934-35 and published his findings in *Food, Health and Income* in 1936. They were sobering: fully 30% of the population was subsisting on a monotonous diet (for many school children, lunch was "bread and marg") of low nutritional value. Likewise Seebohm Rountree's study of York, using an extremely conservative poverty scale, shocked many with the extent of the misery it uncovered.

Few Christian thinkers were offering anything approaching specific approaches to the problems. Typical was George M. LL. Davies, MP for Aberystwyth University and the only one ever elected as an explicitly "Christian" candidate. In May, 1936, he delivered a sermon at St. Mary the Virgin, Oxford, on "The Christian Revolution: The Redemption of Unemployment." He stood, he said, between two leisured classes, one having its leisure forced upon it; and the redemption of one is in the hands of the other "through our Lord Jesus Christ." His "Christian social method" for addressing problems was, in addition to being vague, revealing of a very soft definition of socialism. The method "supposes you can only get a harmonious society by remembering and regarding men as personalities with spiritual and physical needs like your own for growth in body, mind and spirit. When we remember this and act on it, we are Christians and also socialists."[86] In the same sermon Davies, a pacifist and author of numerous writings on the subject, could rejoice that "war is arguing itself out of the conscience if not the courts of humanity." Less than two months later, the Spanish Civil War broke out.

The war galvanized the left, greatly raised the temperature of the simmering debate over pacifism, sharpened concern about advancing fascism and provided grist for social Christian mills. *The Church Militant*, e.g., opposed the idea, commonly advanced, that the war represented a

Manichean struggle between Christianity and atheism; a freely-elected government was being attacked by a right-wing revolutionary force and the Spanish Roman Catholic Church had allied itself with reaction.[87] There was no sentimental Romanism among these Anglo-Catholics: "a Papal autocracy is naturally reflected in a Fascist dictatorship." Later, W. F. Hawkins, member of the Leyton Borough Council, wrote that the religious question masked the real fact, that the Church is a rich political party supporting the insurgent Right.[88] Early in the war Hewlett Johnson led a delegation of Christians to Spain, much to the disgust of the Archbishop, who was generally critical of the Dean's political partisanship. Order of the Church Militant member Olga Levertoff joined the delegation and came back optimistic that the government would win. She thought it was taking constructive social measures and displaying order, discipline and an awareness of its purpose.[89] Some social Christian thinkers, sharing Levertoff's enthusiasm for the Republican cause, chided the Prime Minister's neutrality which, they thought, simply played into fascist hands. Others, like Reckitt, sided with Baldwin and attempted to see good and evil on both sides.

While the domestic economic horizon began to brighten the international horizon darkened and the attention of everyone was consequently drawn increasingly toward developments abroad. *Christendom* noted that Anglican pacifism was growing, confident and aggressive in 1936 but, although some who wrote for it identified with the pacifist position, the journal regarded it as an unresolved issue in moral theology and appealed to the Church not to let the debate tear it apart. In perilous times, a united witness was needed. *Christendom* was critical of ordinary left-wing internationalism, a hangover, it felt, from nineteenth century liberalism. But the journal had little to offer in its place, beyond urging the church to preach the "natural" brotherhood of all people under God; the actual juridical form of that brotherhood was left up to the statesmen. The journal also reflected a controversy raging in the nation about the League of Nations. Demant scored it as a "quack promise" and felt it should "crash." Widdrington defended the League and the sense of the Christendom Group's Moreton Conference was with him.[90]

The journal found space for commentary on South Africa, a factual, calmly critical analysis of the government's racial policy; author W. Ranford foresaw protracted conflict in that nation. There was also mention of the Jarrow unemployment march, the most famous, although one of the smaller marches of the period. Unlike *Church Militant*, however, *Christendom* stopped short of recommending catholic participation in similar exercises (the last was mounted in November, 1936).[91] The lion's share of the journal's space continued to be filled with theological reflection, including a surprisingly polemical piece by George Every, taking to task "the new school of theologians" who ponder "the romantic vision of a resuscitated Middle Age where the Pope might wield the two swords in a merry world."[92] He was wide of the mark in tracing this current of thought back to Charles Gore but accurate in his depiction of two contemporary types of what I would call repristination: one doctrinal (new-Thomism), the other socio-political (the *respublica Christiana*). The most telling criticism of *Christendom* thinking was put forward by Ranford: there is no ideal of social reform in Thomas at all, nor was the medieval Church interested in it.   Ranford's article was prefaced, not surprisingly, by an editorial disclaimer!

A matter of journalistic nomenclature cropped up in 1936 that might be of interest to American readers. *Christendom* mentioned that it was aware of a U. S. magazine bearing the same name and edited by the famous ecumenist Charles Clayton Morrison. Reckitt thought their views were similar diagnostically but divergent prescriptively. He and Morrison had apparently discussed the problem - the American claimed he was unaware of the British publication when he revived the name of a magazine put out some years previous under *Christian Century* sponsorship - and had resolved it amicably. Morrison promised to market his version in England on only the most "casual" basis.

Meanwhile, Reckitt was peering anxiously into the future: what we have presently, he thought, is not peace but "an armistice protracted through eighteen wasted and tormented years, and not destined, it would seem, to last much longer."[93] The younger generation doesn't know about war and its members rush ahead "to the doom that seems so irrevocably prepared for them..." Reckitt's 1936 timetable included an attack on Czecho-Slovakia by Germany in 1938 and war on its eastern frontiers by 1940. He was sure Christian opinion would support, in the event, an "honestly defensive war;" he was less sure about one of intervention.

Reckitt, Peck, *et al.* returned constantly to the theme of a dogmatically clarified and strong Christianity providing the basis for a new social order. Other thinkers, if they were unable to take secular, pluralistic society with sufficient seriousness, nevertheless offered analyses that made more modest claims for the church. One such was W. F. Lofthouse. "Most people are agreed," he wrote in 1936, "that society is facing to-day one of the most serious situations in its history."[94] But he criticized the discussion of the crisis in ecclesial circles. The assumption, Lofthouse thought, seemed to be that the original task of the church was to transform the whole structure of social life and this assumption is wrong. There is no way to move directly from the teachings of Jesus to social principles. The church is charged instead with inculcating precepts, being salt and leaven in an age dominated by what he called Eudaemonism. The burden of his argument, which has a clear apologetic dimension, is that Jesus never expected the church to triumph or for Christian ideas to predominate. Therefore the church should not be held accountable for failing to produce that which lay outside the intention of its Lord.

Another thinker who was interested in appealing to the disaffected, albeit with a theological method quite different from Lofthouse's or from his brother philosopher A. E. Taylor's was John Macmurray, Professor of the Philosophy of Mind and Logic at the University of London. His 1936 Terry Lectures at Yale reflected the crisis of which Lofthouse wrote, a crisis that challenged religion, in Macmurray's judgment, to abandon its conservatism and its support for reactionary movements and to adopt an empirical stance. For Macmurray, "the personal is the fact of central importance" and his writings, marked by meticulous reasoning and an elegant style, exemplify the widespread interwar interest in psychology. This emphasis on the personal in relation to the Other, however, does not mean, for Macmurray, that religion is a purely private affair. It cannot be defined as Whitehead's "what an individual does with his solitariness" but must serve to strengthen "fellowship and community."[95] His master concern was the creation of a society that values equally freedom and equality, with religion as the catalyst. He felt that in modern scientific culture, fact and value had been pulled apart, a theme familiar in the work of Temple, and that the "religious intention" was needed to bring them back together.[96] He joined the *Christendom* editors in heaping much praise on the Middle Ages, although he nowhere called for a return to medieval religious forms. For Macmurray, religion is expressed not so much in doctrinal systems as in a "spirit" which binds people together in a common enterprise toward large goals. Already in 1933 he nominated Nietzsche and Marx as symbols of the paths society could take: one, the fascist, that kills "faith in freedom and equality," the other, the socialist, which sets the spirit free.

With many, Macmurray waited "with breathless interest" for the results of the Marxist experiment in Russia. His 1935 book on the subject is marred, however, by the presentation of a theoretical view of communism out of close touch with actual developments in the country.[97] Since freedom and equality represent, for Macmurray, the "essential core of real belief in God," he could view communism at aiming toward godly ends.[98] It is the ends, the overarching, qualitative, humanistic goals, that a society should keep before itself, he felt, thus coming closer to *Christendom* in spirit. And if many Anglo-Catholics would not share his enthusiasm for the new Russia, they did join him in his summons to a "definite, detailed and circumstantial" assault on the existing social structure.[99]

One of those Anglo-Catholics, Kenneth Ingram, wrote the widely-read *Christianity - Right or Left?* In 1937, in which he seconded Macmurray's call for the church to go with the flow of the future, i.e., to the left. "This is an age of crisis," he wrote, surprising no one, "a relentless hurricane of unsettlement which uproots tradition and undermines faith." The need is for leaders to prepare for "the coming upheaval," which was discernible in the teetering capitalist system. It was, for Ingram, "a movement which arrives at its own self-destruction." The need for good leadership was underscored by the enchantment simple notions, like Social Credit, had for many. Ingram was critical of the "advanced conservative" thinkers, like Harold Macmillan and other in the Next Five Years group, who, he thought, were fully aware that a crisis exists but thought disaster could be staved off by centralized planning within the capitalist system. The liberal progressivism and modified socialism of William Beveridge, *et al.* Ingram viewed as utopian: there would be no way for a plan to be uniformly enforced. The only alternative to capitalism he could envision was socialism. Bipolar thinking was a prominent feature of Ingram's writing - he tended to be taken captive by his antinomies - but it was a weakness he shared with many other writers in the thirties.[100]

Capitalism, according to Ingram's theological analysis, is at odds with the social teaching of Christ. It fails to appreciate the value of each person as a child of God, evaluating them solely by the criterion of wealth. It promotes control of the many by the few, contradicting Christ's dictum "neither be ye called masters..." And capitalism emphasizes national sovereignty, which militates against the Christian ideal of a united humanity. For its continuation, some form of fascism is necessary, the evils of which could readily be seen in Nazi Germany where, Ingram wrote, 35,000 people were held in concentration camps. He was aware of the Jewish agony, but emphasized his belief that the internments were for the crime of expressing proscribed political opinions and he betrayed no inkling of the Final Solution.[101]

Ingram devoted a section of the book to a survey of the Church of England. He gave high marks to the Archbishops but felt that they were exceptions among the clergy, who propounded generalities and shrank from politics. He identified the main stream of Anglican social theology as that

running from Westcott through Copec and from Copec into the Christian
Social Council, the League of the Kingdom of God and the Summer School
of Sociology. Another, smaller stream had its headwaters in Stewart
Headlam and was represented by the Catholic Crusade (Ingram failed to
take note of its transmutation into the Order of the Church Militant the
previous year) and by the Socialist Christian League. His sympathies lay
with the more radical, political tradition and he was critical of Reckitt and
his friends for their "need of aloofness" from other, secular groups, thus
weakening Christian impact.[102] They were, he said, suspicious of the left
because of its non-religious coloration (he could have added its tendency
toward collectivism) and were openly hostile to the Soviet Union. His
analysis of *Christendom* was apt on the whole and leaned only slightly in
the direction of hyperbole: "Industrialism becomes the real enemy, and
affinities are readily discovered with such panaceas as Major Douglas's
credit theories, or with distributism - a return to a small-holding agricultural
community, or a revival of the craft guild. It indulges in theories much
more than in contacts with the working classes, and the romanticist streak
is the price of this policy of aloofness."[103] And he feared that the logic of its
position would lead it, "as the world-crisis matures," to come down on the
fascist side.

Ingram's ecclesiology left no room for the idea that the church should
develop its own peculiar body of social thought. It must, rather, work for
social improvement with secular allies, believing "that the left represents
the fulfilment of Christian values on the plane of action." God can use
movements outside the church for his purposes. Indeed, Ingram could be
said to have preached an extreme form of apologetics, showing the secular
world, especially the left, that its best instincts represent what Christianity
was so haltingly aiming at all along: one senses the "anonymous Christian"
idea here, later developed by Karl Rahner.

Ingram himself was moving, if not outside the church, at least outside
Anglican orthodoxy. His principal guide in this journey was Macmurray
and his "realist religion" is much like the latter's empirical faith. He comes
the closest of any writer of the period to a purely pragmatic or
instrumentalist view of the church[104] and with his evolutionary cast of
mind[105] and lack of stress on sin, he seemed more like an American social
gospeler, in his later years, than did any of his colleagues. Like them, he
often fell back on vague generalities, although he could suggest that what
the church needed was a modern order of preaching friars who would go
about advocating Christian social principles. The habit: flannel trousers and
a pullover (his sartorial suggestions did not extend to summer wear).

The Order of the Church Militant which, along with the SCL was viewed favorably by Ingram, was more inclined to cooperate with the secular left. Jack Bucknall, in *The Church Militant*, urged members to work with communists, socialists and the ILP while keeping their own counsels. He observed that the Stalin-Trotsky controversy was tearing the left apart; the magazine favored convening an impartial international socialist tribunal to weigh the evidence against Trotsky.[106] Like Ingram, the magazine was inclined to interpret events in Russia in a favorable light. In April, 1937, e.g., it opined that the Soviet government had become more liberal toward the churches which, in any case are harmless. But that summer it expressed alarm at reports of Russian tyranny and Noel for his part was always at pains to separate the "real" Marx from what his Soviet followers had made of him. Still, the magazine had space in November, 1937 for an article by F. H. Amphlett Micklewright praising Ingram and Macmurray and referring to the USSR as "the most Christian of countries."

More centrist Christian social thinkers were also busy in 1937. E. L. Mascall, one of the Young Turks of the Christendom Group, issued what amounted to a pep talk, *Death or Dogma*, calling like-minded folk in the church to continue to insist on the corporate nature of human life that flourishes best with cooperation, not competition. A somewhat more wide-ranging essay was penned by Reckitt as a complement to the previously mentioned *Christianity and the Social State* by W. F. Lofthouse. *Religion and Social Action* echoed the dominant mood: stalemate, crisis, fatalism. The author was concerned with "the cult of the future" which asks people to sacrifice themselves to "impersonal causes" which results in totalitarianism, "the revenge of scepticism."[107] He favored the League of Nations but feared it would evolve into a superstate, just as he was unhappy with government intrusion into every sphere of life. As for the church, its primary task is education, keeping the basic issues before the public, for which he praises the "little known" Christian Social Council. Hilaire Belloc was still on the scene, contributing a book whose title, *The Crisis of our Civilization* was vintage thirties and whose content was vintage thirteenth century.

Meanwhile, the ardent medievalists at *Christendom* were complaining that the journal had now found its natural audience and it was small and not growing. An appeal for support went out, an appeal that would echo in its pages the rest of its life. On the substantive side, it continued its thorough promotion of Berdyaev, looked with joy at the recent upsurge in strikes (Kenyon thought this might set the stage for national guilds) and reflected a difference of opinion, underscored by Ingram, in its own ranks. Some thought Christians should do explicitly "Christian" work on such things as housing reform; other thought explicit involvement with the secular left was important on big issues like the Means Test.

While much of social Christianity was busy developing a social and economic philosophy that was not well-informed by expert opinion, one thinker, Josiah Stamp, was busy attempting to correlate Christian principles with hard economic data. In *The Science of Social Adjustment*, published in 1937, Stamp put forward his ideas about the direction in which Britain should be going, grouping them under the term "regulated individualism."[108] The nation had always been characterized by a high regard for personal liberty, he observed, so there existed no real danger that it would become totalitarian. Yet the question of economic planning and, therefore, of regulation, was never seriously in doubt after World War I. The only remaining question, for Stamp, was the shape of the altered order.

Stamp, a world-renowned economist (he held twenty three honorary degrees, including one from Berkeley) and an authority on taxation, was also an active Methodist layman. As such, he was concerned that the economic order not be altered by economics alone but also by Christian teaching. He regarded himself as standing between economics, rapidly disengaging itself from any ethical considerations and the church, eagerly engaging itself with economic matters. He appreciated the work being done on the boundary by Cunningham, Tawney, William Inge and Lindsay, yet "on the whole," he wrote in 1936, "the task is approached by a host of writers and speakers with an excess of sentiment and deficiency of rigorous analysis from the one side, and with too strong an element of scepticism and practical religious apathy on the other."[109] While he wanted to bring economics and religion into conjunction, one of his virtues lay in pointing out where Christian principles *do not*, in fact, apply as, e.g., in working out the equation of need with production, which is regulated by the price system. On the positive side, he proposed two questions to be asked of any economic system: does it provide a good environment for the exercise of Christian virtue and does it demonstrate brotherhood and equality?[110] Stamp was unconvinced that the New Testament contains the rudimentary outline of a Christian society and scored ill-informed clerics who thought differently, producing, as they did, "heavy volumes on Social Economics and innumerable sermons on social improvement."[111] Their time would be better spent, he thought, in preaching individual regeneration and in providing the motivation for experts to come up with solutions to social and economic problems. For Stamp, the great work of the church has been and continues to be to lift up the virtues of pity, justice and the separate rights of individuals. It should constantly remind industrialists that the function of industry is service to the community, not monetary gain.

Stamp was wealthy and in some places in his writings, when he is discoursing on the Christian use of money, e.g., one gets the impression that he is preaching to himself. His emphasis on individual moral responsibility caused him to have an insufficient grasp of the systemic nature of evil and he displayed little passion for improving the lot of the poor. Yet his work was a useful corrective to the romanticism prominent in Christian circles at this time: he disliked the "reversion...to small scale and local hand-craft, without power production, international trade and division of labour."[112] An independent thinker like his mentor, Graham Wallas, he contributed to the national discussion informed critiques of both socialism and capitalism, thereby exhibiting a trait scarce in his era, the ability to move beyond stark antinomies. In underscoring the dangers of moving precipitously from exegesis to action, he pointed the way toward the *media axiomata* position of the World Council of Churches; and social Christianity would have been stronger and more socially salient had it heeded his call to economic realism. Indeed, Stamp was closer in outlook to the architects of the "middle way" than were many social Christians, right or left, and therefore walked with firmer step on the path that led to the actual Great Britain of the post-war world.[113]

Lord Stamp was in attendance at the single most important event in social Christianity in Great Britain in the thirties: the Oxford Conference on Church, Community and State. It owed a great deal to the vision and organizing abilities of J. H. Oldham and was in large part a continuation of the Stockholm Life and Work Conference of 1925. The Archbishop of Canterbury presided at the opening session, after which the chair was taken by the great ecumenist J. R. Mott. Its discussions ranged over a variety of topics (education, leisure, health, economics, international relations, church and state) and resulted in an ecumenical breakthrough: the passing of a resolution to combine Life and Work with Faith and Order. It also resulted in the formation of the Council on Christian Faith and the Common Life, which became the British instrument of World Council work.

A great deal of preliminary work had gone into the Conference, including the publication of seven books and the convening of more than a dozen smaller conferences. Several hundred people sent memoranda, studies and suggestions. At Oxford a galaxy of stars was present: Emil Brunner, C. H. Dodd, Otto Dibelius, Hans Lilje, Otto Piper, Tawney, Temple, Tillich and, from America, John Bennett, John Foster Dulles and Reinhold Niebuhr. In addition, two of the five section chairmen were Americans: Henry Sloan

Coffin and John MacKay. Forty countries were represented by 425 discussants (there were 400 visitors and associate delegates, 100 youth), with a preponderance of western, "first world" representation.

The basic theme of the Conference, according to Oldham, was "the life and death struggle between Christian faith and the secular and pagan tendencies of our time." The Christian, declared the final message, written by Temple, must place loyalty to God over the state and recognize also that economic activities stand under divine judgment. They should aim toward increasing fellowship in a society rather than causing a few to become rich while many remain poor. The report took capitalism to task for its cycles of boom-and-bust, its treating humans as commodities and its fostering of hostility between groups, but did not argue for a thoroughgoing socialism. It advocated, instead, that Christians subject all aspects of the economic order, including property and finance, to moral scrutiny, then engage in political and other activities that further humanistic ends. The report deemed it a mistake to battle for the old *Corpus Christianum*, which always involved the church in more accommodation to the world than was healthy, but urged the church to go beyond individualism to confront institutionalized evil.[114]

The concerns of the Conference went beyond economics and included equal educational opportunity, support for disabled persons, anti-semitism and ecology (although the word was not used). And very much on everyone's mind was the worsening international picture, with Niebuhr speaking of a tendency toward self-glorification as the religion of modern civilization, leading to the apotheosis of party or state. The Conference carried forward the moderate, cautious progressivism of the Fifth Report and, particularly in the work of Oldham, laid the groundwork for the social theology of the World Council.[115] Unlike the Malvern Conference four years later, Oxford was regarded as a success, even exceeding, wrote Oldham, the expectations of many. In addition to being an ecumenical event of decisive importance, it gave social Christianity something it had been lacking, *vis.*, wide visibility among average believers of a variety of communions. Its effect did not end with its immediate impact: Ronald Preston, writing in 1980, judged its theological work to have been unequaled in the intervening years.[116]

"We prepare for war," said *The Church Militant* in January, 1938 and the threat of Installment II of the Great War would hang like a toxic cloud over the year's events. Temple worried that British foreign policy was directionless and drifting, cut off from any fundamental moral principle (cf. criticism of the West's recent handling of the situation in Bosnia). In July, he issued a statement, with the support of leading Anglican churchmen, decrying this opportunistic pragmatism and stating his conviction "that the maintenance of international law must, on moral grounds, take precedence of any national interest in the direction of foreign policy and should be its supreme goal."[117] But as the nations beat their plowshares into swords, Temple was busy at home, serving as chair of a committee investigating unemployment. Begun in 1936, the year, incidentally, in which the pioneering polling organization Mass Observation was inaugurated, the committee conducted a detailed study of the problem in six districts, using funds provided by the Pilgrim Trust. The results of the investigation were published as *Men Without Work* in 1938 and the volume met with warm praise. It illustrated the movement in some social Christian circles away from airy theorizing and toward greater reliance on scientific research as an important component of ethical reflection. Mowat calls it quite "the best social study of unemployment made in the thirties."[118] Among the study's results was the organization of some 1,5000 occupational centers and the extension of Workingmen's Educational Association-style classes and lectures to larger groups of the involuntarily leisured. In a broader sense, Temple's report, along with others', brought home with great force to the public consciousness not only the fact of, but the many evils spawned by, mass unemployment. Such work, then, "provided the launch-pad for the social reconstruction of the Second World War," writes John Stevenson. "It threw into relief what still remained to be done [and] fueled all the aspiration for social improvement and the desire to produce a better society."[119]

The Industrial Christian Fellowship, which stood in the emerging "research" tradition, was also concerned with unemployment in 1938. For failing to provide enough work so that a person's sense of vocation might find proper expression, "the modern capitalist, economic and industrial system must stand condemned," asserted ICF director Kirk.[120] Yet in spite of the swing toward hard data, a certain dreamy vagueness continued to appear in Kirk's work. He could assert, e.g., that "Christianity alone" could provide a social order approximating the ideal; therefore church folk "should set in motion their own social action, and invite men and women of Christian persuasion, in the various political camps, to join them in laying the foundations of a new society which shall be in accord with the mind of Christ."[121] Kirk, however, cited no specifics of such an enterprise, contenting himself with rhapsodizing about the new society, based, somehow, on love, in which "men's material and spiritual needs would be fully met, because by acknowledging and accepting the Divine Purpose and

Plan, things would fall into their rightful place." When he did attempt specificity, he violated Stamp's canon of informed analysis with a wholesale indictment of the financial system, which wickedly conspires to maldistribute the abundant products of factory and field. To his credit, Kirk kept fundamental theology clearly in view and recognized the difficulty of applying broad biblical principles in the ambiguity of concrete instances. And he voiced a fear that has only grown in intensity with the passing years: how will human beings retain their humanity, their freedom and integrity, in the face of advancing technology?

Another major figure concerned with the effect of technology on civilization was John Middleton Murry. In 1938 he was arguing that the machine, that "monstrous and awe-inspiring instrument of perpetual change," is the distinct product of western Christianity, the pattern for which, in his "outward-going creative activity" was St. Paul.[122] The problem, as Middleton Murry saw it, was that the moral and spiritual strength of Christian society had been sapped, leaving humankind with the means for material progress but without a steady center that holds. Thus the only hope is the recreation of an acknowledged spiritual authority, no less than the "refounding of a Catholic Christendom."[123]

He was one with the *Christendom* tribe in bewailing the dissolution of the medieval synthesis but he did not share its enchantment with neo-Thomism. Never an adherent of any ecclesiastical party, he was, in T. S. Eliot's phrase, a "genuine heretic"[124]who in his earlier years seemed to be a pantheist but later came to believe in a personal God and even took steps toward ordination in the Church of England.[125] He was a respected literary critic in the interwar period, although his influence was often compromised by his penchant for airing his personal (and especially his romantic) difficulties in public. His social conscience having been awakened by reading Tawney's *Equality*, Middleton Murry had been active on behalf of the ILP, but he grew disillusioned with the political arena and withdrew from it after 1933. His work was not wholly theoretical, however. He founded the Adelphi Center, a sort of socialist "commune" where Middleton Murry presided as prophet and priest of his own "religion of love" that owed much to Keats and to D. H. Lawrence. A romantic escapee from Victorianism in the Morris-Ruskin tradition, he stood between those who had given up on the church altogether and those for whom socialism was a new religion; and the vagaries of his thought reflected the indeterminate, fluid character of intellectual life, religious and secular, in the twenties and thirties.

In his communal days, Middleton Murry could be seen as supporting the ruralist approach to (or reproach of) industrialism. A more balanced view of the urban-rural tension was supplied by one of the young generation of *Christendom* fellow-travelers, Douglas McKinnon, in the September, 1938 issue of the journal. His appreciation for the Middle Ages did not lead him to idealize the peasant. Rather, he wrote that we should remind ourselves that farming is an honorable vocation, a fact easily lost sight of in the Machine Age. In an expanding economy, farmers should receive their fair share. It is interesting to note that McKinnon's remarks on justice in the fields occurred in the context of an article on twentieth century English philosophy, exemplifying the journal's consistent attempt to render social judgments naturally grounded in a comprehensive axiomatic system. This system was the basis for a heated jeremiad, poison-penned by Reckitt, against Ingram's *Christianity-Right or Left?* The author, wrote Reckitt, lacks an understanding of the transcendent nature of the church and has no concept of autonomous Christian social analysis deriving from dogma. Therefore he baptizes secular reform movements and makes them absolute. This mucking in the political mire offended Reckitt: are we to make over Christianity so as to be palatable to members of the Left Book Club? he wondered. And he continued: even Conrad Noel's highly charged medievalist project in Thaxted "can't attain to Kenneth Ingram's standards of political activity. We have our differences with Thaxted, but we emphatically prefer the Church Militant to the Church Sychophant."[126]

The Church Militant, meanwhile, was somewhat more favorably inclined toward Ingram's book and it joined *Christendom* in noting the demise of the League of Nations. The former regarded it as a league of capitalist states based only on fear and should never have been supported in the first place; the latter thought it was a false union; true, lasting union is possible only where there exists an underlying unity of faith, values and a common culture. *The Church Militant* was keeping an eye on China, wondering if it would go Red and reprinting an speech by the "revolutionary" Chiang Kai-Shek on "Why Should We Believe in Jesus Christ?" Its eye, too, was on the Soviet Union, with Jack Bucknall urging support for Trotsky and Amphlett Micklewright treating the brouhaha surrounding him as an internal Soviet problem. When it glanced at Germany, it remarked that the "accumulating iniquity of the persecution of the Jews strikes a new note of horror."[127]

All the action was not in the international arena, however. The decade witnessed the eclipse of the private landlord, attended by rent strikes such as the large one at Bethnal Green in 1938 and, the following year, in Stepney, which was led by Fr. St. J. B. Groser, a prominent participant in social Christianity after World War II.[128] In education, the principles of free secondary education and a higher school leaving age were incorporated into the Spens Report. But it was overshadowed by the threat of war and little action was taken. In fact, the educational system changed only slightly during the thirties. Yet change was taking place on a broader scale, in the direction of the Responsible Society, fueled by energies released even before the Great War.

Symbolic of that change was Harold Macmillan's *The Middle Way*, published in 1938. In it, he put forward a key idea and a necessary cause for the construction of the Responsible Society: that economic laws are not graven in stone and that the whole system is tractable to mental effort. The result of this effort is, of course, planning, the object of which is to bring order in the face of "the strangely haphazard and insecure character of our economic position," thrown into bold relief as it was by the financial crisis of 1931.[129] Macmillan acknowledged that the whole notion of planning could be scuttled by critics' attacks on admittedly inadequate proposals; nevertheless, he wrote, "we must advance, more rapidly and still further, upon the road of conscious regulation."

Macmillan wrote as a secular politician. Yet in his writing there are strong reverberations of Christian social teaching. He argued, e.g., that in thinking about the economic order, one should begin with human needs and aspirations, not with theory: "the purpose of economics is to serve life."[130] It is also to preserve personal liberty, a chief value of the utilitarian radicals that became distorted in the more complex context of the Industrial Revolution. Overcoming the distorted individualism of *laissez faire* was an important element in the social Christian crusade and it was taken up by Macmillan in *The Middle Way*. Citing the complexity of the context, he argued that to preserve individual liberty at this point required society "to accept greater communal responsibility for the governance of economic organizations and for the welfare of individuals.[131]

From the vantage point of 1938, Macmillan looked back on a half-century of progressive reform, which produced social services for the poor financed by "the negative procedure of transferring wealth through taxation or levy." But it was time, he said, for this "era of radical reformism" to come to an end in favor of a new era based on positive economic reconstruction. After the hardships and indignities visited upon the unemployed in the Means Test era, the future Prime Minister looked forward to a "policy of greater compensations and lesser sacrifices." Yet he was not prepared to swallow socialism whole, afraid of the submerging of individual rights if it were adopted. Rather, he recommended steering a path between it and the

Manchester School (of conservative economics), between the twin desires for security and freedom. This was the middle way.

In early 1939, *Christendom* was echoing Macmillan's sentiments. The government, it said, must guarantee the "inalienable title to livelihood" to each individual and recover "a natural hierarchy of social values" at a time when 2 million people were still unemployed.[132] Ruth Kenyon, who had been the sole staunch supporter of the left on the editorial board, also shared Macmillan's suspicion of socialism. In its salad days, she wrote, it stood for the rights of the poor and for a healthy corporate life against privatism and it accepted no vague idealism but worked with an intellectually defined method (the last point is debatable). But in 1939, she watched with alarm as the Trades Union Congress grew more and more bureaucratic, the labor movement became more politicized and socialism came to represent either opportunist reformism or dictatorship in the name of the proletariat. Still, Kenyon argued, the left is needed even though it is in disarray.

This disarray was no more evident for Kenyon than in Russia, where the revolution, which she had welcomed, had been betrayed by Stalin. The fall of the Spanish Republic also drew notice, with Berdyaev highly critical of Franco, calling his followers "blasphemous" and the bishops "loathsome." The coming international conflict, however, dominated the journal in 1939. There was no question of its imminence. In September, a year after Chamberlain met Hitler at Berchtesgaden and the British naval fleet was mobilized, *Christendom* declared that "the wrath of the Creator is about to descend" (compulsory military service began in April, the Emergency Powers Act passed in August and war was declared on September 3). The only remaining question was what the Christian posture was to be in wartime. The biggest danger, thought E. L. Mascall, expressing Christendom Group consensus, was that the believer would view his or her own country as an angel of light. The faithful should stay in a state of grace, so as to be able to minister to other wounded in air raids (a form for such ministration was printed in the June number) and look toward cessation of hostilities, when an attitude of forgiveness, not vindictiveness, would be appropriate.[133]

V. A. Demant's 1939 book *The Religious Prospect* picked up, as did *Christendom*, a theme of Macmillan's. Both writers quoted J. S. Mill and both were interested in rescuing what was valuable in liberalism. Demant's interest, however, was theological rather than economic, and he wanted to ground human freedom, *vis a vis* state power, in the *imago Dei*, i.e., in metaphysics. In his view the human mediates between the eternal order (reflected in natural law) and politics and this truth "cannot stand the ravages of the historical weather" if its foundation in Christian dogma is forgotten.[134] He was thus critical of liberal religion in Europe and America (represented, for him, by John Dewey's *A Common Faith*) for giving up doctrinal substance and for elevating "becoming" over "being." Demant dreaded the enthronement of Man and Becoming, which he found in Marxism, with a consequent loss of absolute standards and "the end of real discussion" the result. The rescue of liberalism and hence the salvation of society lay, for Demant, in a return to catholic Christianity, to its profound anthropology and to the divine standard which judges the state by timeless criteria, removed from history.

Shaping society according to timeless criteria was also on the mind of T. S. Eliot in 1939. In *The Idea of a Christian Society* he asserted the need for a social order in which the *natural* end of humans - virtue and well-being in community - is acknowledged for all the *supernatural* end - beatitude - for those who have eyes to see it.[135] Eliot had no idea how such an order was to come into being or what political form it would take. He knew only that a community of Christians, somewhat reminiscent of Coleridge's clerisy, the council of ministers in Calvin's Geneva or the *Republic*'s philosophers, would act as a spiritual and intellectual elite in what, somehow, would be a pluralistic society. This church-within-a-church (he left room for the Church of England) would be a bellwether and monitor, calling society back to the pursuit of its proper *telos* when it drifted away, as it was doing increasingly, in Eliot's view, in the years just prior to the Second World War.[136]

Dr. Hewlett Johnson also wrote a prescription for a sick society in 1939. Unlike the work of the romantic medievalists it displayed no nostalgia for the past; it displayed, rather, a romanticism of collective action teamed with a large fascination with science and technology understandable in an ex-engineer. In *Act Now!* he adverted to his engineering degree and asserted "I know that what Christianity demands as essential, science has made possible."[137] What Christianity demands, for Johnson, was justice, freedom, a creatively abundant personal life and human brotherhood and he devoted many pages to adducing these principles from the Bible. He also thought that the British people shared a common faith which added up to nothing but a "common Christianity": respect for personal freedom and security, the value of argument, objective truth, sense of humor, etc. Upon this faith, Johnson was convinced, a socialist order could be erected, the result being that "the community would shortly grow immensely rich." His model for this "Christian" society was Russia. He granted that "she has inevitably thrown out much of the good," nevertheless "the Russian *principle* at least is Christian and civilized, and the mode scientific." Johnson's portrait of the Soviet state was rosy and glowing, making it seem almost the earthly locus of the Kingdom of God.

In *The Socialist Sixth of the World*, also brought out in 1939, Johnson seemed at pains to let his readers know of his caution in assessing the achievements of communism. "There is a need," he wrote, "to guard against a too rosy and optimistic view of life in the Soviet Union."[138] Nevertheless, it represented for him a new stage in human progress, its noble program falling under the sponsorship of Lenin but meeting unfortunate obstruction from Trotsky. As for Jews, "the world's standing problem," Johnson felt that Russia "has found its best solution." The theological sections of the book were weak, tinged with evolutionary optimism and with the author's judgments about Soviet society sounding desperately naive. Yet, while many writers in the thirties were talking to each other in a closed room,[139] Johnson's Soviet encomium sold over 3 million copies and was translated into sixteen languages.

The decade that began with the threat of financial collapse concluded with the collapse of a fragile peace. The Archbishop of Canterbury appealed for his fellow citizens to prepare to help refugees driven from Germany and the discussion of *justa bella*, punctuated by sharp disagreements, faded out in Canterbury Convocation. Temple and his wife moved to the north wing of the palace at Bishopthorpe for safety after the air raid sirens began to be heard in York. Auden's "low, dishonest decade" ended with a bang.

Edwin Muir looked forward in 1939 as well as back: "The disintegration, though actual, a general emergency as palpable as the wrecking of a ship in which we all sail, is not merely disintegration, but a mode of change, painful, critical, filled with extreme dangers, but containing also the possibility of a new age of society."[140]

Notes

1. C. L. Mowat, *Britain Between the Wars* (London: Methuen, 1955), p. 352.

2. A. J. P. Taylor, *English History 1914-1945* (London: Oxford University Press, 1965), p. 267

3. Taylor, *ibid.*, p. 284, remarks that unemployment remained "strangely remote from the mass of the community;" it was chronic in the north but less obvious in the more populous, affluent south. (The word "affluent" was first used in the 1880s).

4. T. S. Eliot, *Thoughts After Lambeth* (London: Faber and Faber, 1931), p. 32.

5. Report of the Anglo-Catholic Congress 1930, p. ix. Almost the lone exception was Ruth Kenyon's speech on women and the church. She urged them to attend the Summer School of Sociology and to work for justice for the unemployed.

6. Hugh l'Anson Fausset, *The Modern Dilemma* (London: J. M. Dent, 1930), p. 11.

7. C. E. M. Joad, *The Present and Future of Religion* (London: Ernest Benn, 1930), p. 35. A. E. Taylor was making a similar claim at the time, speaking of the sundering of fact from value that he traced back to Kant; see *The Faith of a Moralist* (London: Macmillan, 1930), p. 20.

8. P. T. R. Kirk, *Nazareth Politics* (London: Arthur H. Stockwell, 1930), p. 23. This was not one of Kirk's better efforts.

9. In 1941, Maurice Reckitt wrote of Christian social thought and Demant: "The directions in which it has developed since 1930 in this country, at any rate in Anglican circles, are primarily dependent upon his thinking;" *As It Happened* (London: J. M. Dent), p. 271.

10. V. A. Demant, *This Unemployment: Disaster or Opportunity?* (London: SCM Press, 1931), p. 11. Prefacing a concept with "this" was a peculiarity of the era, employed also by other writers. There was a magazine, e.g., called *This Prosperity*.

11. *Ibid.*, p. 16.

12. *Ibid.*, p.122.

13. Stanley Pierson, *Marxism and the Origins of British Socialism* (Ithaca: Cornell University Press, 1973), p. 172.

14. Looking back at the end of the decade, Reckitt admitted that he and his colleagues, among whom was Demant, had been "too much preoccupied with ideas, and too little in contact with facts;" *op. cit.*, p. 293.

15. Samuel H. Beer, *British Politics in the Collectivist Age* (New York: Alfred A. Knopf, 1966), p. 279.

16. According to the prevailing opinion up to that time, a retreat from "sound money" was unthinkable. When it happened, it was "the end of an age," "the watershed of English history between the Wars." See Taylor, *op. cit.*, pp. 297-9.

17. For a sketch of Christendom history, see Maurice Reckitt, *P. E. T. Widdrington* (London: SPCK, 1961), pp. 93-116.

18. John Oliver says that it "stands for a mood and attitude rather than for a specific and definable body of individuals." See *The Church and Social Order* (London: A. R. Mowbray, 1968), p. 120. Reckitt and Widdrington were clearly the leaders, however, and the same names kept cropping up in *Christendom*.

19. Reckitt felt that the SCF's influence was slight, despite the prestige of its president; see *Faith and Society* (London: Longmans, Green, 1932), p. 160.

20. Paul Tillich, *The Socialist Decision* , tr. Franklin Sherman (New York: Harper and Row, 1977; originally published 1933), p. 27.

21. Cited in Oliver, *op. cit.*, p. 136.

22. In the early years his name appeared as "Berdiaeff." He was part of the Russian emigré community in Parish, in supplying aid to which Widdrington had a large hand.

23. Oliver Quick, *Philosophy and the Cross* (London: Humphrey Milford, 1931), p. 26. In this and other works, Quick kept the apologetic horizon firmly in view. The search for stability in unsettled times is mirrored in his other 1931 offering, *The Ground of Faith and the Chaos of Modern Thought* (London: Nisbet and Co.).

24. H. Riley and R. J. Graham, eds., *Acts of the Convocations of Canterbury and York* (London: 1971).

25. See H. E. Sheen, *Canon Peter Green* (London: Hodder and Stoughton, 1965). Green was a friend of Temple's, also no fan of gambling. The Social and Industrial Commission of the Church Assembly finally brought out a study of the issue in 1950.

26. Philip Mairet, *The National Church and the Social Order* (London: Church Information Board, 1956), p. 122. Mairet opened up among the Christendom folk the idea of the domination of finance, according to Widdrington, *After Thirty Years* (London: SPCK, 1954), p. 9.

27. Reckitt, *Faith and Society, op. cit.*, p. 11.

28. John Orens, *Politics and the Kingdom* (London: Jubilee, 1981), p. 19. Orens points out that Stewart Headlam's theology similarly combined the sacramentalism of the Tractarians with the social gospel of Maurice; but Gore's impact on the church was far greater than Headlam's.

29. William Temple, *Nature, Man and God* (London: Macmillan, 1934), p. 405.

30. Temple was associated with a group called The New Commonwealth: A Society for the Promotion of International Law and Order. It advocated an international police force and tribunal, with all military weapons placed in the hands of an international authority. The foundation of all this was to be a strengthened League of Nations.

31. This citizenship was demonstrated in his sermon opening the ill-fated Disarmament Conference in Geneva in March, 1932.

32. *Christendom*, March, 1932.

33. Edwyn Bevan, *Christianity* (London: Thornton Butterworth, 1932), pp. 204-210.

34. J. T. Ward, *Chartism* (London: Batsford, 1973), p. 156. Stanley Pierson, *British Socialists* (Cambridge: Harvard University Press, 1979), p. 30, remarks on the tendency of Morris, Carlyle and Ruskin to retreat into historical fantasies.

35. Pierson, *op. cit.*, p. 227.

36. H. E. G. Rope in *Flee to the Fields* (London: Heath Cranton, 1934), p. 195, Sidney Pollard sees some of the same rural escapist impulses in the early cooperative movement; see *The Cooperative Ideal-Then and Now* (London: Rochdale, 1980), p. 3.

37. Percy Dearmer, ed., *Christianity and the Crisis* (London:Victor Gollancz, 1932), p. 12.

38. *Ibid.*, p.53.

39. *Ibid.*, p. 103.

40. Some of the principles on which the Welfare State was founded were outlined in 1933 by A. E. Garvie in *Can Christ Save Society?* (London: Hodder and Stoughton), p. 192: physical necessities guaranteed to all citizens; state responsibility for the sick, aged and young; a living wage; education for all. Garvie registered his shock that food was being destroyed to keep up prices, when many were hungry; this motif recurs repeatedly in a variety of authors in the period.

41. *Christendom*, June, 1933.

42. Sidney Dark labeled Buchman an "unpleasant American" and his movement, which became Moral Re-Armament, "the Salvation Army in evening dress."

43. *Christendom*, March, 1933.

44. W. G. Peck, *The Social Implications of the Oxford Movement* (New York and London: Charles Scribner's Sons, 1933), p. 83. Here Peck is in conflict with the more temperate view of Clive Binyon, who thought that the Oxford Movement could be interpreted to favor various styles of piety, thought and action.

45. *Ibid.*, p. 231.

46. *Ibid.*, p. 304. A more sober assessment of the church's role in society was presented in the U. S. the previous year by A. D. Lindsay and published as *Christianity and Economics* (London: Macmillan, 1933). Denys Munby's not altogether untrue review: it "does not say much." See *God and the Rich Society* (London: Oxford University Press, 1961), p. 159.

47. Oliver, *op. cit.*, p. v. Another treatment, less tendentious, of the Oxford Movement was written by Kenyon in N. P. Williams and Charles Harris, eds., *Northern Catholicism* (London: SPCK, 1933). Yet she, too, saw the social aspects of the Tractarian Revival embodies in *Christendom*, in 1933 at the height of its influence.

48. Julian Symons, *The Thirties* (London: The Cresset Press, 1960), p. 47.

49. William Temple, *Christianity and Communism* (London: SCM Press, 1933), p. 13.

50. Joseph Needham, *Time, the Refreshing River* (London: George Allen and Unwin, 1943), p. 13.

51. Quoted in Robert Craig, *Social Concern in the Thought of William Temple* (London: Victor Gollancz, 1963), p. 89.

52. Sidney Dark, *Not Such a Bad Life* (London: Eyre and Spottiswoode, 1941), p. 214.

53. *Christendom*, December, 1934.

54. It is a credit to the integrity of *Christendom* that it included trenchant criticism of its stance on this crucial point. George Every argued, in the December, 1934 number, against striving for the "grand scheme" and in favor of "makeshift alliances" with non-catholics for social change.

55. The journal was also concerned at this time with its study circles, a popular form of social interaction of the day. Progress was being impeded by "the propagandist zeal of the Catholic Crusaders" and their favorable disposition toward Russia."

56.   Lord Hugh Cecil, W. R. Matthews, F. R. Barry, Wilfred Knox, *Anglo-Catholicism Today* (London: Philip Allan, 1934), p. 68. Cecil, Matthews and Barry were outside the movement.

57.   Knox's judgment is confirmed in *Where Stands Socialism Today?* , a collection of lectures by various men to the Fabian Society, published in 1933.

58.   Lord Hugh Cecil, *et al.*, *op. cit.*, p. 19.

59.   *The Chronicle of Convocation* (London: SPCK, 1933).

60.   *Church and Slum*, March, 1934. Editor Ivor Thomas also wrote on housing for the Fabian Society.

61.   J. B. Priestley, *English Journey* (London: Wm. Heinemann, 1934), p. 314.

62.   The model for women career workers in the Church of England was Rosamund Essex. See her autobiography *Woman in a Man's World* (London: Sheldon Press, 1977). She was a prime organizer of the 1935 Albert Hall meeting.

63.   A useful treatment of the women's movement, showing some Christian involvement in its beginnings, is Marian Ramelson, *The Petticoat Rebellion* (London: Lawrence and Wishart, 1967). More than half a century would elapse before the English Church took Matthews' views seriously.

64.   V. A. Demant, ed., *Faith That Illuminates* (London: Centenary Press, 1935), p. 22. He made this same argument in 1933 in *God, Man and Society* (London: SCM Press), p. 42. In *Faith* he gives evidence of wide acquaintance with secular economic and financial authorities and is at continual pains to show how complex the questions are; yet he vigorously defended the simplistic Douglas notion. Demant, an honorary member of the American Academy of Political and Social Science, was in touch with and critical of the writings of Charles Beard, A. P. Sachs and Will Durant.

65.   Demant, *op. cit.*, p. 103.

66.   The pamphlet was part of a series on the "New Economics" to which Ezra Pound also contributed a defense of Social Credit. Johnson's ardor for it cooled at decade's end.

67.   Maurice Reckitt, *Religion and Social Purpose* (London: SPCK, 1935), p. 73.

68.   Edwin Muir, *Social Credit and the Labour Party* (London:Stanley Nott, 1935). For an account of his odyssey out of and back into socialism and his "discovery" at age fifty six that he was a Christian, see *An Autobiography* (London: The Hogarth Press, 1954).

69.   Robert J. Scrutton, "This Prosperity" (pamphlet, n.d., probably mid-thirties).

70.   Cyril E. Hudson, *Preface to a Christian Sociology* (London: George Allen and Unwin, 1935), p. 115. He was still writing of the undue power wielded by the financial interests during World War II. See *Nations as Neighbors* (London: Victor Gollancz, 1943), p. 85.

71.   Mowat, *op. cit.*, p. 432.

72.   Cited in Julius F. Hecker, *The Communist Answer to the World's Needs* (London: Chapman and Hall, 1935), p. 144. The book's sections on religion are twaddle. Hecker had no firm grasp of contemporary Christian trends - he overestimates, e.g., the strength of the Catholic Crusade - and was interested in

religion only as it related positively to class struggle; see *Religion* (London: John Lane, 1935); he did hear, correctly, the "distinct apologetic note" in religious writings of the day (p. 73).

73. John Lewis, Karl Polanyi and Donald K. Kitchin, eds., *Christianity and the Social Revolution* (London: Victor Gollancz, 1935), p. 27.

74. *Ibid.*, p. 102.

75. *Ibid.*, p. 196.

76. A balanced essay by W. H. Heaton-Renshaw, "A Christian Looks at Communism" was published as a pamphlet in 1935 by the Anglican Evangelical Group Movement. The AEGM was a counterweight, in the Free Church direction, to the Church Union. It sought to "relate the Gospel to contemporary problems" and "work for a Christian civilization, founded on the radical social and economic implications of Christ's teachings" but its influence was slight.

77. Kenneth Ingram, *The Coming Civilization* (London: George Allen and Unwin, 1935), p. 205.

78. Malcolm Spencer, *Economics and God* (London: SCM Press, 1936), p. 8. The Interim Report on Unemployment of the Church Assembly's Social and Industrial Commission, issued in 1935, was not as judicious: it gave much attention to Social Credit (Reckitt and Widdrington were members of the Commission).

79. William Temple, *Christ and the Way to Peace* (London: SCM Press, 1935), p. 12.

80. There was even some internal tension: only two editorial board members, Reckitt and Demant, advocated Social Credit.

81. *Green Quarterly*, Spring, 1934.

82. *Ibid.*, Summer, 1934.

83. John Stevenson, *British Society 1914-45* (London: Penguin Books, 1984), p. 186. The chief feature of economic activity in the decade was the boom in housing construction. See Mowat, *op. cit.*, p. 485.

84. Noreen Branson and Margot Heinemann, *Britain in the Nineteen Thirties* (London: Panther, 1973), p. 206.

85. Anne Fremantle, "Balm in Gilead" from *Poems 1921-1931* (London: Swan Press, 1931), p. 25.

86. George M. LL. Davies, "The Christian Revolution: The Redemption of Unemployment" (unpublished manuscript, National Library of Wales, 1936).

87. *The Church Militant*, November, 1936. The small but vocal Catholic Crusade had disbanded the previous month at its annual chapter in Burslem. The divisive issue was Russia, the majority desiring sharper criticism of it. This group was led by Conrad Noel and formed itself into the Order of the Church Militant, also known as The New Society.

88. *Ibid.*, January, 1937.

89. *Ibid.*, May, 1937. *New Green Quarterly* carried articles on both sides of the Spanish Civil War issue as well as on pacifism. The final issue of the journal was published in Spring, 1937 ("killed by the Depression") and readers were invited to

transfer unexpired subscriptions to *Christendom*.

90. *Christendom*, March, 1936.

91. Church halls were opened for marchers along their route but most hunger marches were under communist auspices and thus unlikely candidates for broad-gauged Christian support.

92. *Christendom*, December, 1936.

93. *Ibid.*

94. W. F. Lofthouse, *Christianity in the Social State* (London: Unicorn, 1936), p. 9

95. John Macmurray, *The Structure of Religious Experience* (New Haven: Yale University Press, 1936), p. 23.

96. John Macmurray, *Some Makers of the Modern Spirit* (London: Methuen, 1933), p. 8.

97. It is also marred by a very limited grasp of Buddhism and Islam.

98. John Macmurray, *Creative Society* (London: SCM Press, 1935), p. 24. Interest in radical alternatives to society as it was was reflected in the spectacular success of Victor Gollancz's Left Book Club, begun in 1936. It sponsored political discussion circles, with membership running around 50,000 and mass rallies, at the first of which Hewlett Johnson was on the platform.

99. Kenneth Ingram, *Christianity - Right or Left?* (London: George Allen and Unwin, 1937), p. 17.

100. For a fine survey of many of the celebrated "leftist" writers of the thirties, see David Smith, *Socialist Propaganda in the Twentieth Century Novel* (London: Macmillan, 1978). Smith finds himself almost ready to agree with George Orwell's judgment that the novels were "dull, tasteless and bad" and grants unqualified praise only to Lewis Grassic Gibbons' trilogy *A Scots Quair*.

101. Ingram, *op. cit.*, p. 87. Ingram, like Tillich, spoke of the romantic element in fascism.

102. *Ibid.*, p. 147.

103. *Ibid.*

104. Kenneth Ingram, *The Night is Far Spent* (London: George Allen and Unwin, 1941), p. 63.

105. This is most fully illustrated in *Christianity, Communism and Society* (London: Rider and Co., 1951).

106. *The Church Militant*, March, 1937.

107. Maurice Reckitt, *Religion and Social Action* (London: Unicorn Press, 1937), p. 32.

108. Josiah Stamp, *The Science of Social Adjustment* (London: Macmillan, 1937), p. vi.

109. Josiah Stamp, *Motive and Method in a Christian Order* (London: Epworth Press, 1936), p. 13.

110. Josiah Stamp, *Christianity and Economics* (London: Macmillan, 1939), p. 33.

111. Josiah Stamp, *The Christian Ethic as an Economic Factor* (London: Epworth Press, 1926), p. 18. Many of the ideas in *Motive and Method* were adumbrated in this volume. Stamp was close in spirit to the great American economist John Rogers Commons, who labored for incremental reform through the legislative process and who dropped his involvement with the social gospel in 1895, largely due to fatigue with preachers who could denounce iniquity but had little to offer on the positive side save windy generalities. See Bruce Wollenberg, "John R. Commons and the Social Gospel" (unpublished master's thesis, Indiana University Library, Bloomington, 1975).

112. Stamp, *Christianity and Economics, op. cit.*, p. 141. In a footnote and in the index, Reckitt is "M. D. Rickett."

113. Tragically, Lord Stamp did not live to help shape that world *in situ*: he was killed by a direct hit in an air raid, in the bomb shelter of his estate, in 1941. His biography is by John H. Chapman, *Lord Stamp* (London: Humphrey Milford, 1942).

114. J. H. Oldham, *The Churches Survey Their Task* (London: George Allen and Unwin, 1937), p. 96.

115. Oldham's writing has a "modern" flavor to it and he was one of the first to grapple explicitly with pluralism. See *The Resurrection of Christendom* (London: The Sheldon Press, 1940), p. 30. This sense of living in a post-modern world comes through strongly in Nils Ehrenström, *et al.*, *Christian Faith and the Common Life* (London: George Allen and Unwin, 1938), which came out of the Conference.

116. Ronald Preston, "The Question of a Just, Participatory and Sustainable Society" (pamphlet reprint from the *Bulletin* of the John Rylands University Library, Manchester, Autumn, 1980), p. 96. Thinkers with a high level of interest in social questions were present also at the subsequent Faith and Order Conference in Edinburgh, including Demant, Macmurray, Tawney, Kirk, Raven, Basil Matthews and Eliot.

117. F. A. Iremonger, *William Temple: Archbishop of Canterbury* (London: Oxford University Press, 1948), p. 385.

118. Mowat, *op. cit.*, p. 483.

119. Stevenson, *op. cit.*, p. 295.

120. P. T. R. Kirk, *The Cross and Society* (London: Industrial Christian Fellowship, 1938), p. 6. Kirk was not alone in this; long-time National Guilds advocate S. G. Hobson, e.g., criticized Parliament for simply registering decrees made by the financial powers. See *Pilgrim to the Left* (London: Edward Arnold, 1938), p. 269. Hobson, a leading figure in the old Socialist Quaker Society, wrote for *New Age* but parted company with editor Orage over Social Credit.

121. *Ibid.*

122. John Middleton Murry, *Heaven-and Earth* (London: Jonathan Cape, 1938), pp. 8-13.

123. *Ibid.*, p. 19.

124. Cited in Rayner Heppenstall, *Middleton Murry* ((London: Jonathan Cape, 1934), p. 16.

125. F. A. Lea, *The Life of John Middleton Murry* (London: Methuen, 1959), p. 133. He was in close touch with Christian social thinkers through something called The Moot, an ecumenical discussion group convened by Oldham and including Vidler, Dawson, William Paton, Eliot, Needham and Karl Mannheim.

126. *Christendom*, March, 1938.

127. *The Church Militant*, December, 1938. The magazine was also interested in personal moral issues: Gladys Keable argued for trial marriages while J. Wilson wrote that the normal method of conception control for Christians was abstinence but for others, artificial means were acceptable. (The Family Planning Council, founded on the work of the famous fossil botanist Dr. Marie Stopes, was established in 1938).

128. Another prominent figure in housing reform was Fr. Charles Jenkinson, a political activist in Leeds who was instrumental in the removal and replacement of many of that city's notorious "back-to-back" row houses.

129. Harold Macmillan, *The Middle Way* (London: Macmillan, 1938), p. 9.

130. *Ibid.*, p. 14.

131. *Ibid.*, p. 26.

132. *Christendom*, March, 1939. The journal paid tribute to the memory of T. C. Gobat, unwavering CSU socialist and "one of the stalwarts of the last generation;" it also noted the untimely death of Fr. Rosenthal, one of the new.

133. The journal, beginning to experience graver financial problems, hung on through the war; when it ceased publication in 1950, James Casserley, one of its more insightful writers, then founded *Faith and Society* as the "successor and spiritual heir" of *Christendom*.

134. V. A. Demant, *The Religious Prospect* (London: Frederick Muller, 1939), p. 43. The author acknowledged his great debt to T. E. Hulme, particularly his stress on original sin. Dorothy Sayers was also among those emphasizing the importance of basic doctrine at this time. See *Strong Meat* (London: Hodder and Stoughton, 1939).

135. T. S. Eliot, *The Idea of a Christian Society* (London: Faber and Faber, 1939), p. 27. Eliot's static, non-progressive social order resembles T. E. Hulme's "constant society." F. R. Barry was another author writing at this time of the crucial need for a "Christian society." See *Convictions* (London: Nisbet and Co., 1939), p. xii.

136. A highly critical, almost hysterical view of Eliot, centering on his "proto-fascism" and anti-semitism, is in Russell H. Robbins, *The T. S. Eliot Myth* (New York: Henry Schuman, 1951). It is the case that Eliot's 1934 *After Strange Gods* is not wholly free of the latter vice.

137. Hewlett Johnson, *Act Now!* (London: Victor Gollancz, 1939), p. 17.

138. Hewlett Johnson, *The Socialist Sixth of the World* (London: Victor Gollancz, 1939), preface. This was a Left Book Club selection.

139. See Arthur Marwick, *The Explosion of British Society 1914-1962* (London: Pan Books, 1963), p. 82.

140. Edwin Muir, *The Present Age From 1914* (London: The Cresset Press, 1939), p. 182. Muir made a useful distinction between writers who see *society* in danger (socialists, communists) and those who see *civilization* in danger (liberals, religious thinkers).

Chapter 4

Off Again to Battle

A discussion of Christian social thought between the wars naturally spills over into the forties, principally because of one word: Malvern. This was the last great conference on Christianity and the social order and was viewed by some, in fact, as a maladroit attempt to reinvoke the spirit of the Copec halcyon days. It met in wartime January 7-10, 1941 under the sponsorship of William Temple, who had given major responsibility for the intellectual shape of the gathering to *Christendom* writers. The Industrial Christian Fellowship and its director, P. T. R. Kirk, were in charge of bringing together the 23 bishops, 8 deans and 200 clergy and lay conferees at Malvern. Unlike Copec, where discussion had flowed freely, Malvern was marred by a frenzied schedule of heavyweight speakers, each offering enough material for a full conference, with little time left for debate. Many were ready to leave after the second day and, although Sidney Dark spoke later of a "Malvern revival,"[1] numbers of people were left with a bad taste in their mouths. John Middleton Murry, e.g., scored the conference for its "atmosphere of complacency, its lack of despair," and thought its chief result was the granting of a mild blessing to the state-socialism already developing under the pressure of war.[2]

Malvern was saved by Temple's masterful summary which, he admitted in an introductory note, represented not so much the conference's conclusions as such but a "convergence" of the previous year's preparatory work. The summary serves as a compendium of the concerns of social Christianity in the interwar years. The most controversial issue involved ownership of principal industrial resources. Sir Richard Ackland had proposed that private ownership was wrong and a stumbling block to the moralization of society. Temple's text fudged the issue, asserting that private ownership *may be* a stumbling block.   Otherwise, the recommendations were clearly congruous with mainstream Anglican social thought and with the Fabian progressivism characteristic of the time.

In the published proceedings, Temple defended Malvern against the charge that few experts were invited to the deliberations. If you have only experts, he wrote, you will have a type of fascism: amateurs are needed for balance (Christian social thought, as has been pointed out, was weakened by amateurism). He also responded to the charge that such conferences are exercises in futility. In the period between the wars, the penal system was reformed in a Christian direction, Temple argued; secondary education was extended to much larger numbers of people and the building of proper housing was undertaken on a great scale...all of it done with strong church support.[3] Temple thought Malvern had more theological depth than other conferences.   Delegates were interested in hammering out (under *Christendom* influence) a comprehensive social philosophy grounded in the faith, whereas Copec's approach had been more piecemeal. Malvern also paid more attention to the church itself, both to the importance of liturgy and to the need for putting its own house in order financially. And Malvern took place in an improved society: sweat shops had been abolished, unions accepted, strides in education taken. The main concern now, Temple wrote, is the status and security of the employed.[4]

An indication that Christian social thought had reached the end of an era can be seen lying behind Temple's hope that Malvern would prove a stimulus for church circles to draw together Christian thinking on social issues. This should be done, he suggested, *even if there is little new to be said* (emphasis mine).[5] If Christian social thinkers had sometimes been wide of the mark in diagnosis and treatment and had been preaching, often, to the convinced, they had been busy and they had covered the bases. Temple's other remark about Malvern's hoped-for effect had an apologetic ring: through it, the world would be reminded of the Christian social tradition and of a church that cared about more than simply saving souls.

The conference resulted in the publication of a monthly, *The Malvern Torch*, edited by Sidney Dark. But its most enduring legacy was to be seen in Amsterdam, in 1948, at the founding of the World Council of Churches.[6] J. H. Oldham had written of *media axiomata* in the preparatory volume to the 1937 Oxford Conference and the search for moral direction between laying out broad principles and proposing specific legislation was kept carefully in view at Malvern. Following Malvern, those to the left of the *media axiomata* position formed the Council of Clergy and Ministers for Common Ownership, which early experienced internal controversy over what the group's stance on the Soviet Union would be. Having changed its name in 1952 to the Society of Socialist Clergy and Ministers, it entered into discussions with others, including R. H. Tawney and people from the Socialist Christian League, out of which came *Papers from the Lamb* in 1959 and the new Christian Socialist Movement. Another organization that carries on bravely the tradition of the "little societies" within the Church of England is the Jubilee Group, begun in 1975.[7]

Some thinkers continued to publish during the war: Reckitt (a history of the movement from Maurice to Temple), L. S. Thornton, T. M. Heron,[8] Oliver Quick and William Paton.[9] The ICF carried on, as did the Social and Industrial Commission of the Church Assembly.[10] True to form, Temple wrote the most significant addition to the wartime conversation in 1942, coincidental with the Beveridge Report, to the shape of which Temple had contributed and on which his book was the theological commentary. *Christianity and the Social Order* was immensely popular, quickly selling 130,000 copies (its third edition was issued in 1950).[11] The volume was unthinkable, apart from the often brilliant, sometimes erratic, always passionate work of the advocates of a Christian social and economic philosophy who had gone before. Their work in great part was overtaken by events and it was left to a new generation to rethink social Christianity in a society shaken by new shocks, but which had, at last, come to see itself as responsible to the many and to the least of these.

Notes

1. Sidney Dark, *I Sit and I Think and I Wonder* (London: Victor Gollancz, 1943), p. 37.

2. John Middleton Murry, *The Dilemma of War* (London: James Clarke and Co., 1942), p. 22. Others prominent at Malvern were Peck, Demant, Dorothy Sayers, Mackinnon, Mascall, Matthews, Tissington Tatlow, Ackland and Ingram. Widdrington was unable to attend and Reckitt was ill; his paper was read by Temple.

3. *Malvern 1941 - Proceedings* (London: Longmans, Green, 1941), p. 217.

4. *Ibid.*, p. 220.

5. *Ibid.*, p. 223.

6. Stanley Evans, *The Social Hope of the Christian Church* (London: Hodder and Stoughton, 1965), p. 229. Evans was a leading figure in Christian socialism after the war.

7. Ronald Preston, *Church and Society in the Late Twentieth Century* (London: SCM Press, 1983), p. 26. In the fifties, the most visible social Christian figure in the English Church was E. R. Wickham. He was critical of the church for paying homage to its prophets while ignoring their message. See *Church and People in an Industrial City* (London: Lutterworth Press, 1957), p. 212.

8. Heron, an industrialist, wrote an endorsement of the Beveridge Report for the ICF, *The Relation of Freedom and Control in Industry* (London: ICF, 1943).

9.   His *The Church and the New Order* (London: SCM Press, 1941), with its extensive quoting of Oldham, clearly reflects the emerging ethos of the WCC.
10. The commission published a study of gambling, as mentioned in the previous chapter, in 1950; already in 1948 an Archbishops' Commission brought out *The Church and the Atom.*
11. It was not, as might be expected, received with universal acclaim. Sir Lennox Russell published a diatribe against it, *Coercion or Voluntarism?* (pamphlet issued by The Discussion Groups Association) in 1944; it was a dying gasp of nineteenth century *laissez faire.*

Index